Reflections from Africa

Chad D. Northington

Reflections from Africa

Copyright © 2011 by Chad D. Northington

International Standard Book Number: 9780615269344

Library of Congress Control Number: 2008911866

All rights reserved. Except for use in any review, the reproduction or utilization of this work in whole or in part in any form by any electronic, mechanical or other means, now known or hereafter invented, including xerography, photocopying and recording, or in any information storage or retrieval system, is forbidden without written permission of the publisher.

Scripture quotations are from:

The Pocket Bible, *Today's New International Version* © 2005 by Zondervan Corporation. Used by permission. All rights reserved.

For information:

Visit http://www.transformationalministries.com

Printed in the United States of America

To my wife, Tiffany, who has taught me how to love deeper and live happier.

TABLE OF CONTENTS

CULTURE SHOCK AND THE SEARCH FOR IDENTITY 1
    REFLECTIONS ON PURPOSE..21
    REFLECTIONS ON ETERNITY..23

CULTURAL ASSIMILATION AND INTERNAL TRANSFORMATION 25
    REFLECTIONS ON TRANSFORMATION 48
    REFLECTIONS ON FAITH 50

OUT OF THE CULTURAL HONEYMOON AND INTO PERSEVERANCE ...54
    REFLECTIONS ON PERSEVERANCE 68
    REFLECTIONS ON SERVICE 70

REVERSE CULTURE SHOCK AND UNDERSTANDING COMMUNITY 72
    REFLECTIONS ON COMMUNITY 88
    REFLECTIONS ON RELATIONSHIPS 92

INTRODUCTION

This book is but one story among a vast collection of stories around the world that have remained relatively untold. They are stories of ordinary individuals striving to change the world for the better with what resources and abilities they possess. Their passions and motivations may differ, but they all see hope for a better tomorrow. In a world where the media thrives on reporting news of war, destruction, politics and tragedy, it is difficult to find such stories - and such hope. I wish to tell you that such hope exists, the world can be changed for the better and you can have a part in it.

Several years ago my wife and I embarked on an incredible journey that eventually led us to Cameroon, Africa where we served with the national church in providing clean water, health care and hope to the Cameroonian people. During our time there, we stood before kings, sat with lepers and slept with refugees. We are ordinary people following extraordinary commands to love our God and love our neighbor. This book is a collection of cultural and spiritual reflections gathered over the course of our first year in Africa. It is my hope that they will serve as encouragement, instruction and entertainment for anyone considering an experience in the developing world in the role of a Christian development worker, humanitarian or missionary. I am not going to describe the methods for installing a hand dug well or treating malaria. However, the application of these skills and others were vital in fulfilling our desire to reach the unreached and provide for the physical, spiritual and social needs of those who needed it most.

I am a Christian; it is what both defines me and motivates me. By profession, I am an environmental engineer driven by a desire to preserve our planet as a steward of God's creation. I do not draw a line between my secular career and my religious beliefs; they serve one another synergistically. I am an environmental engineer gone missionary with a heart to reach the unreached. I have come to the very simple conclusion that I cannot claim to be a Christian and not feel compelled to actively do something about the state of the world. We all have a decision to make. When will we stop waiting for change and instead become a part of it? I made the decision, and that is why my wife and I found ourselves living across the ocean in a small African community where basic needs, such as water, health care and food, are still a daily concern. No, they are more than that. They are a struggle.

We all have our own world view, and it is this world view that determines what our "better tomorrow" would look like and how we believe we can (or cannot) achieve it. My world view describes a tomorrow where there will be no death, no pain, no suffering and no mourning. Poverty will be vanquished, and justice will rule supreme. There will be everlasting water, food, joy and love. That is the hope in me that fuels my passion to create such a world new to the extent possible in a place that is plagued by what Christians refer to as sin. The world has fallen and needs to be picked up again.

This book is neither a debate on theological issues nor a philosophical discussion. I have neither the academic background nor the authority to make claims in these realms. This book, however, is reality. It is not a fictional portrayal of an attempt at world change; it is a collection of actual experiences and insights over the course of our first year in Africa as seen through the fresh eyes of a couple who had never spent an extended period of time overseas. Perhaps it would be best to consider it a practical guide for those considering a different path. My hope is that it would inspire and encourage those who want to take the next step towards that better tomorrow and would like a glimpse of what that has looked like for someone else.

That sense of there must be something more, something better seems to be everywhere. Many are yearning for an escape from an intangible enemy that has enslaved us to materialism, consumerism, relativism and individualism. The threat of global disaster or annihilation seems to grow closer with each passing day. Global climate change, wars, famines, water shortages, genocide, economic uncertainty, natural disasters impacting millions – the list goes on and on. We know something has to change but what and how? What are we to do as individuals in the face of such looming peril? I say our part. If we all do our part, we can change the world together one act at a time, one day at a time and one life at a time until over 6 billion people have been cured of their illnesses and freed from their suffering. It begins with relationships – our relationships with one another, the environment and our Creator. They are all broken and need to be repaired. Every single day we are faced with the choice of how we will address these aspects of our life. A simple change in attitude, lifestyle and priorities can lead to a whole new world.

    I would not dare to claim that I possess the perfect formula for world peace and meeting everyone's basic needs. I would dare say it begins with a right relationship with God. Our entire life changes when we become accountable to someone or something else besides ourselves. When we devote our time, energy and talents to something greater than ourselves, a passion is ignited. It becomes an unquenchable fire that consumes everything around us. If we believe eternity exists beyond this life, we have no choice but to live differently. If we believe we will one day stand before our Lord and Savior Jesus Christ, as I do, and give an account of how we spent this life He has given us, we have no choice but to listen to how He said we should live it.

    I do not expect that your idea of truth falls perfectly in line with my own. It does not have to in order to appreciate what my wife and I have experienced while trying to live out our truth in a place where we felt we could have the most impact given our prior experiences, training and passion. What is important is that you understand we are average Americans that had just as much, or little, to lose or gain by venturing on this journey to do our part. We are not independently wealthy, we did not grow up in model families and we have made our share of mistakes. We are by no means saying that everyone should sell their belongings and head off to an unknown land in order to accomplish world change. What my wife and I would say, though, is that you need to identify where it is you can have the most impact and then go! It may be in the African bush, but it is more likely that it is next door or in your local community. It is not uncommon in our day and age to not even know our own neighbors, co-workers or even our own family well enough to impact their lives in a positive way that can ultimately lead to world change and a better tomorrow.

      Whatever your situation or your idea of truth, making the world right is a calling we all share. What good is knowledge of any truth if we do not live it and share it? The very essence of truth is that there can be only one, and some of us will be closer to it than others. As a Christian, I believe that truth was revealed and lived in the person Jesus Christ through whom we came to understand what perfect humanity could look like. Humanity, as a whole, has the same general sense of right and wrong in regards to issues such as social equality, justice and preservation of life. If it did not, we would live in a world of utter chaos. The time has come to stop waiting on the world to change and to start changing it. It is time we devoted our lives to something greater than it.

CHAPTER 1

CULTURE SHOCK AND THE SEARCH FOR IDENTITY

DECEMBER 17, 2007

    It has been nearly a week since our departure from the States. Our period of adjustment has gone well, and we are all moved into our African home for the next year. We have already witnessed a miracle here – all seven of our bags arrived intact and on the same flight in Yaoundé, the capitol of Cameroon. We can't say the same for our last flight into the country during a brief two-week visit to prepare for our long-term commitment. One of our plastic totes arrived two days late in a plastic airline bag and a million pieces. We were especially concerned this time because we were asked to bring two boxes of HIV test reagents for an organization that attempts to prevent the transmission of HIV/AIDS from pregnant mothers to their infants. The fragile shipment was on ice, so any delays or damage would have been a significant loss. It's difficult to get supplies of any sort into the country, and sometimes the best way to transport such articles is to send them with visitors on commercial flights.

    Our first full day in country was spent negotiating the price of items we would be unable to purchase once we arrived at our new home in the more rural environment of the Adamawa Province about twelve hours away. Shopping is always quite the experience because there are no stores that resemble the supermarkets we are familiar with in the States, and generally everything is negotiable. Tiffany had the easier task of pointing out the desired item, and I had the pleasure of doing the "dance of negotiation" with my broken French. Because I had relatively no idea what the going rate is for most things, I'm sure we left several happy vendors in the market. I did manage to upset one woman who was trying to sell us some vegetables. Apparently my offer was completely unreasonable based on her use of the word *voleur* (i.e. thief) in her response. There's no better orientation to a country than spending time in the market environment.

We flew out the next day loaded down with our luggage, bags of food, supplies and that one item I couldn't do without – coffee. I was a little nervous on our way to the airport. It wasn't due to the videogame-like drive there where every turn felt like it could be your last and random objects and people seemed to be everywhere; it was due to the anxiety of knowing we could be overweight for our bush plane flight and may have to leave behind certain "non-essential" items, like coffee for example.

Driving in Cameroon is an adventure in itself. If you're an adrenaline junky, this is the place for you! The only rule on the road it seems is there are no rules. Well, actually there is one based on several close calls – pedestrians do not have the right-of-way. It will definitely take some adjustment to get used to the driving "technique". I thought moving from the laid back highways of Michigan to the congested expressways of Florida was a change for this former Michigander…

After our arrival at the hangar, we weighed ourselves and cargo. I was relieved to discover we had about 20 kilos (i.e. about 45 pounds) left, but we had definitely cut it close. Our pilot turned out to be a fellow Michigander who was preparing to go on furlough back to the Great White North. The world certainly does become smaller the more you travel. I couldn't even imagine going from the tropics of Africa to the tundra of the Midwest. We found the weather in Cameroon to be much like that of Florida this time of year, so fortunately that was one adjustment we didn't have to worry about. We had arrived in the dry season and won't see the heavy rains until around March. When I say dry, I mean dry! There's not a drop of precipitation for months, and a thin film of red dust covers everything.

Tiffany seemed more relaxed than I had expected during her first "bush plane" flight based on the nap she snuck in while cruising at 7,000 feet in the 5-passenger aerial taxi. Our hour and a half flight was a great way to see Cameroon. The alternative would have been a minimum twelve hour ride by what they refer to as "bush taxi", and the chances were the current road conditions would have turned it into an overnight trip. Maybe next time...

We arrived at our destination with a greeting committee waiting for us on the grass landing strip that doubled as a grazing pasture for the local sheep and goats. It felt like we were coming home even though our previous stay earlier that year had been short. The community of Banyo is like a breath of fresh air compared to the hustle and bustle of the capitol city, which seems almost unrepresentative of the rest of the country. But Cameroon is surely a country of amazing diversity in all respects – peoples, language, religion, climate, geography, you name it. In that respect, the capitol was very representative. Cameroon is often referred to as "Africa in miniature" because of how well it represents the rest of the continent in its geographic and ethnic diversity. It's hard to appreciate the vastness of the African continent. We currently reside in a country the size of California, and it is only a fraction of the continent's surface area.

Our first night was spent in conversation with our new family. There are two other American couples in our community. We were excited to see a new addition to the local hospital since our last visit, where my wife will be volunteering. The hospital seems to be in a state of constant growth as the demand for health services continues to increase in the area. There will be no lack of opportunities for Tiffany to serve as a medical professional. The same can be said for the water projects and my involvement in this ministry. We are excited about the possibilities and this period of relationship building.

It had been a long road to get to this point, and there was a sense of relief that we were finally standing on African soil with all the hope and energy that comes with a sense of purpose and a mission at hand. I thought back to my first trip to the country nearly 3 years earlier that had put me in touch with the engineer who had started the water ministry I had inherited. He had accomplished a great deal in his thirteen years of water ministry, and I certainly had some big shoes to fill. It took us nearly two years to make all the necessary preparations and raise the required support for a 1-year commitment to serve. We had originally wanted to stay for two years, but the challenge of raising the funds as "short-termers" proved to be more difficult than we had anticipated.

Knowing our time was somewhat limited gave a greater sense of urgency to "hit the ground running". Fortunately we had also inherited a lot of resources from my predecessor that will allow us to begin the work we had come to do rather quickly. I think my previous short-term visits to Africa took away a lot of that initial culture shock one tends to experience in an environment that stands in such sharp contrast to the one from which we have come, which I hope will lessen our period of cultural adjustment.

DECEMBER 20, 2007

    I'm writing today after my first solo adventure in Cameroon. It seems that throughout the country there are small pockets of refugees along shared borders with neighboring countries like the Central African Republic, Chad and others. These refugees go relatively unnoticed in the international media. An opportunity has presented itself to provide a well and living water to a village of approximately one hundred refugees. Many of the refugees scattered across eastern Cameroon have settled in villages which do not resemble the "camps" we are accustomed to seeing on the news. It seems that unless there are hundreds of thousands or even millions affected, we won't see it on the evening broadcast. Nevertheless, the inhabitants of this village have suffered much loss and find themselves displaced in a foreign land. Most of them have migrated to existing villages and blended in with the population. However, the additional members have put a great strain on the village resources.

    This particular people group is known as the Fulani, or the Fulbe, as they would refer to themselves. They are the largest group of nomadic people in the world, numbering approximately 20 million, and are spread all across West Africa. Their culture is distinctly characterized by a code of conduct known as *Pulaaku*, a way of life comprised of strong family and clan ties, fervent adherence to their religion and a pastoral lifestyle. However, for many Fulbe the nomadic way of life consisting of herding cattle had involuntarily come to end, and they now found themselves having to learn a new way to survive. Such was the case for this particular village where the inhabitants had taken on a more sedentary lifestyle dominated by agriculture. Cassava, peanuts (or groundnuts as they call them), hot pepper, corn (locally known as maize) and okra cultivation had replaced the herding of cattle. Many of the refugees who had fled from the Central African Republic had lost their cattle and more in raids by lawless bandits. They were often easy targets when they were encountered in small groups while herding their livestock.

    In order to assess the situation, I joined a local Fulani man for a trip to the village by "bush taxi". If this is a new term for you, imagine a small passenger van from the 1970's full of as many people as you can fit inside. Now multiply that number by two and throw a ridiculous amount of luggage on top. Add a lot of dust, missing parts, a couple of chickens or a goat and a couple of broken windows and doors. Voilà - you have a bush taxi! Of course I couldn't adequately describe the sights, sounds and smells that accompany a bush taxi ride, but I'll leave those to the imagination.

I had my first lesson in African time that morning when I went to catch the taxi. I scrambled out the door with breakfast in hand to make sure I was at the stop by 6:30 a.m. only to discover an hour later that the taxi schedule was a little looser than that to which I was accustomed. When the taxi did arrive, I had the honor of sitting in the front next to the *conducteur*, or driver. At least I thought it was an honor at first. I quickly realized that lacking a seat belt and traveling roads unfit for anything with wheels made me quite vulnerable to a trip through the windshield if something went wrong. I noticed a nice steel cage separated me from the other twenty passengers or so behind me, and it also separated them from the windshield. Seven hours of travel in this environment passed more quickly than I expected as I took everything in and shared brief conversations with a man and his young son seated next to me, but this is certainly not a mode of travel I would recommend to everyone.

Upon arriving at our destination, we were greeted by several of the "big men" in the village. This is a common term used here to describe men of high position in the society. Unlike most Fulbe villages, there was no *jarro*, or chief, to greet. The village was comprised of refugee families who had arrived over the course of seven years united by a common need to survive and a common need for hope. I found the Fulbe to be an attractive people. Their distinguishing features are a more slender, taller frame and lighter skin than many of their African brethren. We spent the first hour in introductions while snacking on dense, fried bread called *makala* along with hot tea and milk. Although it was the middle of the afternoon, I was invited to a bucket shower followed by a period of rest. If you are unfamiliar with the term "bucket shower", it is basically a bath taken with a bucket of water, sometimes warmed, and the bowl of your choice. I was permitted to relax in the one house in the village with a straw bed and corrugated metal roof. The remaining *saare*, or houses, were of mud brick and thatched roof construction typically found in the village setting.

The Fulbe were very welcoming. I was incredibly impressed with the way they carried themselves, and I could see the *Pulaaku* characteristics of modesty, patience and endurance expressed in their behavior. Many of the people groups we had encountered thus far were more forward about their needs, but the Fulbe were quite reserved, which made assessment of their physical needs that much more difficult. With the help of a translator, we were able to communicate back and forth between Fulfulde and my barely comprehensible French. I was far too excited to nap, but I tried to relax for the allotted time.

We spent the afternoon checking flow rates at a couple natural springs on the hillside and determined some potential hand dug well locations. This was followed by a grand tour of the village and more introductions. I had the opportunity to hand out a few balloons to the children, which were a big hit. The need for a good water source was obvious as I evaluated two very contaminated, unprotected spring sources. A variety of activities occurred at the small pools in front of the spring besides the gathering of drinking water, including the washing of dishes, clothing and children. It was also a frequent stop for the local animals.

We spent the evening sharing a meal of fist-sized corn flour dumplings, called fufu, which is by far the most common meal among the Cameroonians. It is eaten with your hand (right hand only as the left hand is reserved for other activities after dinner if you know what I mean) and is usually accompanied by a tomato or okra-based sauce, perhaps with a couple small chunks of unidentifiable meat. Bedtime came quickly, and I was too exhausted to care about the number of six-legged friends who had somehow managed to find their way inside my mosquito net. The gentle pitter patter of other four-legged friends also surrounded me as they investigated the bags of corn piled around my makeshift bed. Probably one of the most uncomfortable things I've experienced so far is the scurrying of a cockroach across my face in the middle of the night.

I awoke to the much more pleasant sensation of singing at about 5:00 a.m. In the darkness and drowsiness of early morning, it seemed almost like a dream. As the music began to crescendo, my senses were awakened, and I realized it was not a dream at all. I stepped outside and found a woman singing while sweeping debris from the ground in front of the compound. Instead of growing lawns, the Fulbe remove the vegetation adjacent to their compounds; the equivalent activity to our lawn mowing is dirt sweeping. The cattle and chickens next to my room were in a similar state of drowsiness it seemed. Had I known the challenges that awaited me this day, I may have just remained in bed...

Tiffany and I had agreed I would try to make this just an overnight trip with this being my first time "away from home". The plan was for me to leave early in the morning by myself, and my traveling companion would depart the following day in order to complete some unfinished business. The plan slowly began to crumble as we realized there would be no bush taxis this morning. An important annual Islamic celebration was underway called the *Feast of the Lamb*.

A quick trip into town led to the discovery that we shouldn't expect a taxi until about 11:30 a.m. In other words, I *might* see one around 1:00 p.m. or even later. We went for a short walk to pass the time and ended up running into a family that would be traveling through our town via an old French Pugeot station wagon. Now I've had my share of lemons, but this one took the cake, even by African standards. I didn't want to miss what may be my only opportunity to reach the next major town, so I jumped in and said a quick prayer. It would appear God wanted to ensure I had the proper orientation to Cameroon when my feelings about the vehicle were confirmed 5 kilometers down the road where we found ourselves stranded.

After about 2 hours of being assured the repair would be completed momentarily, I decided to catch the next bush taxi heading west. This time I didn't get the front seat, but instead found myself positioned on a half seat next to the entry doors. Comfortable wasn't exactly a word that crossed my mind, but at least I was on my way to the next town of Tibati, where I would hopefully find another taxi (and a full seat).

Fortunately, I did find another taxi after reaching Tibati. However, what I didn't know was that it would be another six hours before our departure as they waited for enough passengers to fill up the vehicle following the festivities. I had a lot of time on my hands to observe the activities in town, interact a little with the locals, negotiate for a couple of pineapples and try the local cuisine. I was thrilled to discover they offered a sort of roadside Bar-B-Q, called soya, cooked over wood on an old 55-gallon drum. I am still at a lost to identify all the different parts of the animal I was served. My experience had been that as long as the food is served hot it is generally safe to eat roadside meals even if it may appear unidentifiable.

We finally left around 8:00 p.m. with a nearly full taxi and a 5 hour trip ahead. I thought the roads were bad during the day, but they are infinitely worse at night when the driver struggles to see the next major pit (pothole doesn't adequately describe the road conditions). I felt like I was on a bad fair ride as we were jostled and thrown for five hours. I can't tell you the sense of relief I felt when I finally saw a distant landmark, a local mountain called Mt. Djumbal, bathed in moonlight. I yelled to the driver, *"C'est l'hôpital"* (that's the hospital) and quickly descended, forgetting my handkerchief and loaf of bread in my fatigue and desire to find my bed.

The following morning required several cups of Cameroonian-made coffee to gather my senses following my adventure home. The perfect blend of arabica and robusta coffee beans makes Cameroonian coffee one of my favorites. We are expecting visitors today and will have a full compound, as they call it around here, when the doctor's family arrives from Europe to celebrate the holidays with us. Tiffany and I are now in the swing of things as she has begun work at the hospital and I have begun preparations for water projects in the local community and beyond. We are also experimenting with some of the skills and appropriate technologies we learned in the States prior to our departure, like composting, biosand filter construction, a no-till farming method and small-scale tree production.

DECEMBER 28, 2007

I became intimately familiar with the community today after participating in what I am calling "The Tap Tour". The community receives much of its water from a large gravity flow water system fed by two springs. The water is supplied through a network of distribution pipes and stand pipes that lead to shared neighborhood taps or private taps in the homes of local "big men". The system was designed by my predecessor and officially inaugurated about two years before my arrival. In that short period of time, the system was already at risk of failing catastrophically due to a lack of routine preventative maintenance and the difficulty in collecting the small fees from the community required to purchase materials and pay the monthly technician salary of about 40,000 cfa, or $80 USD.

A technician on the community water team and I visited all of the 30+ water taps in town via a 125cc motorcycle. I would have considered the bike a little small for me alone, but we had two grown men on it. I've seen up to four Cameroonians at a time riding on this common mode of transportation. This might seem possible if the roads were smooth and paved, but they're not. In fact, I witnessed two accidents during our tour. One accident involved a *gendarme* (policeman) dodging a little boy in the road on his own 125cc motorcycle. He ultimately ended up in a ditch and very upset, but no one was injured with the exception of the policeman's pride. The second accident was an overturned semi truck that had rolled off a bridge unfit for most cars let alone a full-size truck. It had been loaded down with hundreds of shelled peanut bags. The open trailer had fallen into the river below, where the bystanders were reaping the benefits of being in the right place at the right time as they stuffed whatever they had with runaway peanuts.

As I suspected, the greatest challenges I will face in assisting with the management and maintenance of the water system here will not be technical in nature but rather cultural. The greatest challenge I observed was the general perception of the community that the system was a gift from the *Nasara* (i.e. white man), and it wasn't necessary to pay the fees. This led to a vicious cycle where the technicians failed to perform their duties because they weren't being paid, the system would fail because the technicians weren't doing their work and the communities refused to pay because they weren't receiving water. I felt a bit overwhelmed by the task at hand.

The first tap stand we visited had been taken offline after I learned that one of the local madmen would attack and destroy it from time to time. In this part of Cameroon, and probably many parts of Africa, there are no facilities where psychologically disturbed individuals are sent and have access to medications for their illness. Instead they are often found wandering the city streets or in the market. They tend to be of no danger to the general population and live off the generosity of others. However, it would appear that they can be a danger to inanimate objects like water tap stands...

The next tap visit was even more interesting. A water line had been run to the local prison, so we took off down a long road to the far north of town. When we reached the tap, we found a lone guard outside a set of large doors leading inside a walled compound. After the usual greetings, we inspected the tap outside the prison and made note of a small leak. I was then informed by the technician that there was another tap inside. Unbeknownst to me, the tap was located right in the middle of the prison. Thinking we were walking into the prison administrative quarters, I was escorted past the large doors and suddenly found myself in a small, crowded courtyard surrounded by about 100 prisoners with the only way out locked behind me.

I nonchalantly inspected the second water tap in the prison yard trying to mask my fear and hide the cold sweat that was forming as the prisoners closed in around me. My tour guide had failed to inform me that this would be part of our inspections, and I had no idea what to expect from this unique entourage of water users. I could only think about the same scenario in the U.S., where I probably wouldn't have had this much time to contemplate the situation. To my surprise, I was soon being greeted with a friendly *"bonjour monsieur"* in French, or *"sannu"* in Fulfulde. A few brief handshakes and greetings allowed me to work my way back to the door where I breathed a sigh of relief on the other side. That particular visit had caught me a little off guard.

Every tap we visited was unique in some way or offered its own maintenance challenge. Because it was Friday, many Muslim men were returning from the mosque and exchanged greetings with us as we stopped at each location. It was an exciting and intimate way to experience the city life in a Cameroonian community. Next time I'll pass on the prison tour, though…

JANUARY 9, 2008

    Today I am writing you from the back of a "bush plane" on our way back following a conference with fellow workers that took place in the much more developed city of Bamenda. If you read my previous description of a bush taxi, you can liken a bush plane to that except it travels 7,000 feet above the ground and doesn't typically include the chickens or goats. The turbulence experienced at that elevation is very similar to that experienced on Cameroonian roads. Tiffany can testify to this after exiting the plane last time with a full sack provided for "motion discomfort".

    I volunteered to take the infamous back seat on the return flight and am anxiously clutching my own motion discomfort sack in the other hand. Our flight was delayed this morning when our pilot had to fly a medical evacuation, so unfortunately that meant we had to take the more turbulent afternoon flight. The visibility is also very poor due to the seasonal Harmattan, an incessant onslaught of dust from the north that leaves your belongings and lungs coated with a fine red dust. I am probably not making the best decision by writing in these conditions, but there are many things I'd like to share about our recent activities.

    Besides fellowship, teaching and training, the conference also provided the opportunity to expand our ministry. For nearly a year we have been in communication with a couple from Cameroon who have started a farm co-operative to support indigenous Cameroonian church workers. They are in desperate need of a good water source for irrigation and drinking. They had already purchased a solar pump and were now looking for assistance with the installation of an appropriate well system to meet their water needs. This is actually not the first time I have met this couple. During an unexpected encounter a few years ago, we were introduced to them through mutual friends while they were visiting the United States. We had no idea at the time that one day we would be visiting them in their own country let alone offering up our services to assist with their ministry. It's truly amazing to witness God's orchestration of events and encounters in our lives.

I was able to make a site visit and believe we will be able to assist them by installing a borehole or hand dug well. When I had arrived, the fuel-powered centrifugal pump they had been using to distribute water from a small stream in the valley was being repaired, and they lacked even a source of drinking water. We hope the installation of their solar pump in a well and the construction of a holding tank will provide a gravity flow network to their home and fields so they may continue providing support to Cameroonian pastors.

Tiffany and I also had an opportunity to meet with a Cameroonian pastor we have been supporting who is working among an unreached people group in the Southwest Province. Like us, he shares our passion for providing for the physical and spiritual needs of unreached peoples through transformational development. We have joined others in assisting with the necessary funds to send him to training in South Africa that will provide courses in integrating discipleship with community development.

I am looking forward to our return to continue our ministry both in the local community and in the surrounding remote "bush" areas. The water team is diligently working on many needed repairs of the community gravity flow water system so that we may focus our efforts on the opening of a community outreach center for the promotion of appropriate technology, health education and the Gospel as well as begin preparations for test drilling in a refugee village in Eastern Cameroon.

Tiffany will continue her medical ministry at the hospital and also hopes to accompany me during our work among the refugees. Water and medical care are the primary physical needs in this area, and we hope to assist with both. No one in the village has access to medical care, so even simple assessments could be life-saving if problems are identified before they become too serious. The size of the refugee village is expected to double shortly following the report that a delegation of refugee representatives from the Central African Republic visited the village and expressed the desire to join them.

Although I'd like to write more, I think I will be risking "motion discomfort" in about another paragraph.

JANUARY 19, 2008

This entry comes to you from a small refugee village in eastern Cameroon where we have begun test drilling in preparation for a hand dug well installation. The test drilling is done with a small, hand-operated drill rig to verify the depth to the water table and to confirm the absence of any obstructions that would hinder digging. The village we are working in is the same one I described previously, which consists of approximately 100 Fulbe refugees from the Central African Republic.

Tiffany and I have been able to team up with this refugee ministry. While I work with the drilling crew, she is performing health screenings of the village's sick through a "bush clinic". A bush clinic is essentially a local hut that has been turned into an examination office for those in need of medical attention. If the likely cause of the illness can be identified, medications are prescribed according to a program established by the national church with whom we are partnering. It has only been a half day of consultations and she has already seen tape worm, amoebic dysentery, malaria, asthma and multiple cases of "belly bite", as they refer to conditions that cause stomach aches. The state of some patients is far too severe for diagnosis in the bush, and they are referred to a facility where they can receive more advanced treatment.

As often seems to be the case in Cameroon, getting here proved to be half the challenge. In order to transport the drilling equipment and several people, I rented a bush taxi for the day. This meant squeezing six people, baggage and all the tools into a car the size of a Toyota Corolla. In fact, it was a Toyota Corolla! We decided to also have two people travel by motorcycle in order to ease the load and add a little comfort to the ride for the other passengers. Of course I had no reservations about jumping on a dirt bike and accompanying one of our team members, who also took his own off-road bike. With the dry season in full effect, we had to tie bandanas around our faces and wear sunglasses to avoid death by dust suffocation. We looked like a couple of modern outlaws on our steel horses. I figured that after traveling by bush plane and bush taxi, it was only natural that I attempt travel by "bush motorcycle". It seemed to me that a dirt bike may be the only mode of transportation fit for such road conditions.

As we began our journey, I had one of those moments where I felt I was right where I was supposed to be. Bouncing along an African road on a dirt bike on my way to do God's work with a clear sense of purpose was a great feeling. My moment of spiritual ecstasy was short-lived when my traveling companion pulled off the road with a flat tire. Fortunately this is a common occurrence in Africa for which he was well prepared. Tiffany and the others passed by as we prepared to remove the tire tube. We tried to flag them down to let them know what had happened but they just drove by waving to us as if everything was O.K. It's a good thing the situation wasn't life-threatening or I probably wouldn't be here writing this!

We repaired the tire and were off in no time. And in no time we found ourselves in the same situation. This time, though, I had been leading and had gotten a little further ahead of my traveling companion than I should have. I stopped at the next rendezvous location and waited several minutes before realizing something had happened. I jumped back on my bike and sped back down the road.

Many African countries are rather infamous for the *gendarmes*, or roadside police, and the corruption that lingers at these roadside stops. Unfortunately Cameroon is no exception. One can be stopped at anytime for any reason by a gendarme. This time it happened to be my turn. On my way back through the police checkpoint, I was flagged down and signaled to pull aside by a piercing whistle blow. The officer sternly asked me for my papers in French and took little time to inform me there was something wrong with my paperwork. Consequently I was asked to step off the bike and have a seat.

In my broken French, I tried to explain I had a friend who was in distress and needed my aid. My plea, however, was insufficient to convince the gendarme that my emergency was more important than the fact I did not have my 2007 sticker for the motorcycle. In Cameroon, drivers must purchase a small *vignette* sticker every year, which is basically a tax on the vehicle. Keep in mind that it is now 2008 and the motorcycle had not been ridden by me or anyone else for that matter in 2007.

The 2008 sticker wasn't going to be available for another month, which I learned when we tried to purchase one in Banyo.

My attempts to explain this were futile, and I sensed a rational explanation was not what the gendarme was seeking. He then began to offer me "options" through a series of questions like, "Do you want me to write your name in this book and take you to the judge?" It was becoming quite evident that if I had really done something wrong these things wouldn't necessarily be at my discretion.

Tiffany and the others finally showed up after what seemed like an eternity of interrogation by the officer. They indicated the other bike was down the road a bit and everything seemed fine, as he was having a conversation with someone nobody recognized. I was thinking I had gone through an awful lot of trouble for him to be having a random conversation with a stranger, and I still wasn't off the hook.

I informed our other team members of my predicament, and they insisted I shouldn't pay anything. That was easy for them to say; they weren't the ones being threatened with fines or jail time! Apparently thinking everything was O.K. (or not wanting to get more involved), my friends, including my wife, jumped in the bush taxi and continued off to their destination.

I realized I was still stranded and needed to make some decisions. I approached the gendarme again, and he casually asked, *"Vous avez réflichi?"* This meant, "Have you thought about it?" I had, and I told him 2007 had already passed. This meant, "I'm not paying your bribe and take me to the judge if you want." Apparently my response was enough to indicate he had lost this battle to fatten his pockets. He handed me my papers, and I returned to the rendezvous spot where this had all begun.

I prepared to recount my tale to inform my friend of what had passed during his chit chat with strangers. Upon his arrival, I was informed he had actually had another flat tire, and a stranger had stopped to help. When he tried to wave down our friends in the bush taxi, they just waved and smiled as they passed! At least I wasn't the only one abandoned in my time of need...

FEBRUARY 3, 2008

I have begun to realize that after over a month of living in Africa that there are a number of things that not so long ago seemed quite strange to me but now have become either part of the daily routine or lack that same bizarre quality they once possessed. Take the kitchen, for example. I've really acquired a taste for powdered milk, the only kind available around here. The bowl of floating fruits and vegetables in the sink is just our disinfection process where we add small amounts of bleach to prevent any irregular digestive activity. Speaking of which, it is no longer inappropriate to talk about dysentery, amoebas, worms or the like at the dinner table. The use of voltage regulators and transformers for what few electric appliances we do have is also the norm now as we attempt to protect our belongings from the regular surges and power outages common in a place where intermittent electricity was typically not available when you really needed it. Our counter has become a model for recycling, where empty glass bottles, used aluminum foil and reusable plastic bags lay scattered as they dry for yet another use. It is also in the kitchen that I now often find myself asking how animals and insects that were once inedible would taste fried.

There are still quite a few habits I struggle to break, though. Probably the most costly has been the often fatal mistake of plugging a 110-volt device into a 220-volt socket. It's not fatal for me, of course, but it has been fatal for the computer battery and cordless tool chargers I brought along. May they rest in peace. I am also trying to break the habit of arriving at church, or any event for that matter, early or on time. I think it has something to do with the fact that the church service can last 4 or more hours. This is partly because the sermon has to be translated into at least one other language. I carry two to three different Bible translations with me every Sunday. It makes for great language study but a long church service.

I have realized that my futile attempts at the necessity of respecting time and other people's time have fallen on deaf ears. And speaking of time, the days of receiving letters in a couple of days is a thing of the past; try a couple months! Even when we write the date, we don't know whether to write the day first and month second or month first and day second. The clocks that we do see tend to confuse us anyways, as they follow a 24-hour time format. Time has lost much of its meaning, as we now tend to measure it differently. For example, if you're driving somewhere, you ask how long it will take to get there rather than how far it is. And if you are driving somewhere, remember there is <u>always</u> room for one more person, animal or bag.

We also don't miss many of the creature comforts as much that we had been accustomed to in the States, except soft toilet paper that actually rips along the perforations of course. I definitely don't miss the television, as we didn't watch much of it back home anyways. We now have something much better – shortwave radio. Irregular power is no longer seen as an inconvenience and more like a normal part of life in Africa. I do miss my dog, however. In a country where rabies is common and they sometimes eat dogs, I thought it was best that she stay with family at least for our first term overseas.

It's a strange feeling when you live somewhere and don't truly feel like you fully belong to the culture, but at the same time don't feel like you could ever fully belong to the culture from which you came. That's sort of where we're at after over a month in our new environment. Submersion in another culture reveals a great deal about who we are at the core of our being. All our previous cultural expectations are stripped away and the only thing left is you – the real you, whether you like it or not.

I've found the one of the greatest challenges in our cultural "assimilation" is hanging on to those qualities from our own culture that bring out the best in us and letting go of those that bring out the worst. For myself, the American sense of initiative and hard work can go a long ways in Africa, but the resultant project-oriented, impatient attitude is a stumbling block to real progress and real relationships, which are vital to all aspects of life in Cameroon. Likewise, we strive to acquire the positive aspects of our new cultural environment. A relationship-oriented approach to life changes how everything is done, from greetings to business. My hope is that in time we will represent the best that both cultures offer and live a life that is more Christ-like than it was when we only knew of one way to express our cultural identity. Fortunately our spiritual identity is not dependent upon our geographical or cultural position.

REFLECTIONS ON PURPOSE

As a Christian, I find my purpose, my identity, my vocation in being a steward of God's creation and a servant to others. Until the arrival of Jesus Christ on this planet, we could not fully understand what God or humanity was to look like. In the person of Jesus Christ, we found perfect humanity reflected in his words and actions.

In a society that often seems ruled by things like materialism, individualism, relativism, corporate greed and self-gratification, our greatest challenge may be to turn from a self-centered world to a God-centered world where we seek His will for our lives and not our own. This task becomes easier as our will begins to fall in line with God's will for our lives, and the mold formed by society begins to shatter. A new mold is formed that is shaped by the Word of God rather than the word of man. Our minds and hearts are transformed, and, consequently, so are our actions and attitudes.[1]

Of course as Christians we do not "work" our way into heaven – eternal salvation is a gift of God given freely to those who put their faith in Him.[2] However, we also know our faith without works is dead.[3] Our goal should be to actively live out our faith in word <u>and</u> deed as we strive to be more Christ-like.[4] God does not want part of us; He wants all of us. Our time, energy, talents and resources are gifts from Him to be used for Him. Our love for God is expressed in our obedience to His commands. His love for us is expressed in the sacrifice of His Son for our sins.[5] Living a life that follows these commands has significant consequences both in this world and the next. At the core of these commands lies love – love for God and love for one another.[6]

As far back as I can remember I have believed in a greater good and being a part of something bigger than myself. I have always felt we are all entitled to the most basic of needs, such as clean water and food, and without fulfilling these needs we could never achieve greater aspirations such as world-wide health care, education or peace. This life philosophy shaped me during my young adulthood and led me to a career in environmental engineering. It also created a desire to help those I believed needed it the most – inhabitants of the developing world. A series of events in my life resulted in a heart for the people of Africa.

It was not until a few years ago, however, that I realized meeting only physical needs was not enough. As human beings, we require much more than just food and water; we require love, relationships and an understanding of our origins, purpose and destiny. We were given the perfect demonstration of how we are to love one another and God. Jesus Christ came to this world with a purpose and a mission that was lived out daily in every encounter as he met both the physical and spiritual needs of the people. Every encounter was another example of Jesus identifying a need and providing for it. We see how through the performance of a miracle or communication of the right words, lives were transformed. Everything Christ did was to glorify God the Father.

Likewise, we should consider every encounter an opportunity to share God's love and provide for the needs of another child of God. We have been offered the greatest gift that could ever be offered – eternal life.[7] And there is no greater purpose or mission in this mortal life than to share that news with those who do not know it and to continue to build the kingdom of God through our actions until it is completed in all its glory.

REFLECTIONS ON ETERNITY

Individuals who possess an eternal perspective on life and understanding of our role in it have no choice but to live differently than the world with its desires. Rather than focusing on accumulating treasure on earth, they strive to build up heavenly treasures.[8] These may be intangible treasures in this life, but they serve as the currency for the next. In a culture that seeks sure investments for the future, this sort of investment has often been overlooked.

An internal compass guided by a sense of eternity and accountability results in a much different way of living than one guided by the lusts and temptations of this world. When we begin to live with an eternal perspective, we also begin to see ourselves as a much larger community, God's community, where we are all brothers and sisters with different gifts and abilities to contribute to the family. I believe it is this defining perspective that forms the very foundation of conduct for every human being. There is an incessant struggle waging between the mortal flesh with its temptations and lusts and the eternal spirit. The choice we make between the two will determine our place in eternity.

Besides placing a sense of eternity on our hearts, God has also made us aware of eternal consequences for our choices.[9] Scripture states that we will give an account for what we have done with our lives.[10] Our time on this earth is like a blink of an eye compared to the eternity that awaits us when we finally open our eyes. Yet this brief mortal encounter is all we have to reach out to our Creator and seek His grace and forgiveness. Our thoughts, actions and choices will determine our place in eternity. Such a mindset adds a sense of urgency to finding the truth ourselves and then sharing it with others once we have embraced it.

In the Gospel of Matthew, Jesus asks, "What good will it be for you to gain the whole world, yet forfeit your soul? Or what can you give in exchange for your soul?"[11] We must treasure that which is eternal and guard it against the lust and luster of non-eternal desires. When we regard this life as temporary and our possessions as blessings instead of belongings, we realize what we have is a gift from God to be used to glorify

Him and not ourselves. Our homes, our cars, etc. do not define us; they are merely instruments to help fulfill the will of God. These things will come and go as "moth and rust destroy", but our soul remains.

---

[1] Do not conform to the pattern of this world, but be transformed by the renewing of your mind. Then you will be able to test and approve what God's will is – his good, pleasing and perfect will. (Romans 12:2)

[2] For it is by grace you have been saved, through faith – and this is not from yourselves, it is the gift of God – not by works, so that no one can boast. (Ephesians 2:8-9)

[3] As body without the spirit is dead, so faith without works is dead. (James 2:26)

[4] Dear children, let us not love with words or tongue, but with actions and in truth. (1John 3:18)

[5] For God so loved the world that he gave his one and only Son, that whoever believes in him shall not perish but have eternal life. (John 3:16)

[6] Jesus replied: "Love the Lord your God with all your heart and with all your soul and with all your mind. This is the first and greatest commandment. And the second is like it: 'Love your neighbor as yourself.' (Matthew 22:37-39)

[7] For the wages of sin is death, but the gift of God is eternal life in Christ Jesus our Lord. (Romans 6:23)

[8] Do not store up for yourselves treasures on earth, where moth and rust destroy, and where thieves break in and steal. But store up for yourselves treasures in heaven, where moth and rust do not destroy, and where thieves do not break in and steal. For where your treasure is, there your heart will be also. (Matthew 6:19-21)

[9] He has also set eternity in the human heart yet no one can fathom what God has done from beginning to end. (Ecclesiastes 3:11)

[10] And I saw the dead, great and small, standing before the throne, and books were opened. Another book was opened, which is the book of life. The dead were judged according to what they had done as recorded in the books. (Revelations 20:12)

[11] Matthew 16:26

CHAPTER 2

CULTURAL ASSIMILATION AND INTERNAL TRANSFORMATION

FEBRUARY 7, 2008

Assimilation to another culture must be one of the most interesting experiences we can have in life. It's like a return to infancy in many ways; we learn how to communicate, eat, dress, etc. all over again. However, we bring an entire history of learned behaviors with us that we may not realize are learned until we are once again forced to think about them.

Take eating etiquette in Cameroon, for example. Among the Fulbe people and others, many meals are consumed without the luxury of utensils. Food is typically spread out in dishes on the floor and eaten family style (i.e. everyone dips into the same plates). Consequently, the food is often something you can roll in the hand and then dip in a sauce. The selection of which hand to use is another important element of eating etiquette. In many African cultures, the left hand is reserved for certain sacred activities, if you know what I mean, therefore food is always eaten with the right hand. You might not think this is exceptionally challenging to remember to do, but perhaps you're not left handed like me. Try eating with your left hand here and see the astonished looks you receive. It's bad enough when they see how I write!

And then there's the matter of language. I had my first large community meeting last night, which I reluctantly conducted in French. Although French is one of two national languages in Cameroon, it is often a second or third language for many Cameroonians. It is not uncommon to find Cameroonians who speak three or four languages fluently and a couple more with less ease. It can be rather embarrassing to be the American who struggles to complete a single sentence in another language without error. My audience in this case primarily spoke the local dialect of Adamawa Fulfulde, so I was speaking my second language to have it translated into a third language. This certainly gave new meaning to "lost in translation".

It was evident from certain facial expressions I observed that much of what came out of my mouth in French was equivalent to the babblings of a three or four year old, and that may even be a rather generous assessment. It's rather humorous albeit frustrating to have so many adult thoughts and child-like communications at the same time. The real mystery is determining what they really heard versus what you thought you said. Fortunately, I had a translator by my side to correct me when I went astray. I was a bit perplexed when I would make a brief statement and my companion would turn it into a full-blown speech. I came to realize that besides translating my words, he also had to communicate the cultural context, and that can take some time.

Let's not forget dressing habits. Tiffany and I both face unique challenges in this category. For me, it's the inability to wear shorts. In a climate that rivals my native Florida for heat and humidity, this is not an easy thing to accept. Shorts are considered acceptable for children or during sporting events. Considering my language abilities, I am probably often viewed as a child and should probably just wear shorts anyways. Tiffany's challenge is the cultural ban on women wearing pants, or trousers, as they call them here (pants actually mean underwear). It is not uncommon for a woman wearing trousers to be regarded as sexually promiscuous. Long skirts, covered shoulders and covered heads are the safest bet if a woman doesn't want to cross any cultural lines.

This list of cultural tidbits could go on and on. Don't cross your legs when you sit. Feel free to talk on your cell phone in the middle of an important meeting (yes, cell phones are everywhere). Don't worry about being on time for anything. Make a funny slurping sound when you drink hot tea. God's diversity in creation is amazing…

FEBRUARY 16, 2008

After two months of living in the relatively remote Adamawa Province, I have returned to the capitol city of Yaoundé to do some shopping, retrieve some funds (it's one of the few places with an ATM) and pick up a ministry vehicle to help with the water work. Going from Banyo to Yaoundé is like traveling from small-town America to New York. The capitol is busy, the air is hard to breath and it's loud, but there is a vast array of activities and people that make it unique in a way like New York is unique in the States.

Much like the Big Apple, it is very exciting if you can avoid being run over by the swarm of taxis running to and fro. Very few Cameroonians can afford their own cars, so the streets are littered with second-hand Toyota Corolla taxis that carry passengers to their destination in a vehicular dance of sorts. A lack of signs, lights, right-of-ways and defined lanes put driving in Cameroon right up there with skydiving and bungee jumping in my book. You sort of feel like you're in a video game, but in this case your life is actually on the line.

There is a sort of art in hailing a taxi unlike that of trying to catch a ride in the U.S. If you want a ride, you motion for the taxi by pointing downward. You then quickly state your destination and the price you are willing to pay as the driver rolls up. Yes, even the taxi fare is negotiable in Cameroon. If the driver disapproves of your offer, he speeds off to the next potential client. Otherwise, he signals his acceptance with a quick beep. There doesn't appear to be a limit to the number of passengers or baggage if the price is right. I recently saw a family of nine, everything they probably owned and the driver crammed into a Corolla like a bunch of sardines.

Shopping here is a bit of a reality check on how much we take for granted back home. It's amazing what becomes a treat when you're in a developing country. There are several "upscale" shopping centers in Yaoundé for the city's elite and expats. To give you an idea of what I mean by "treat", here's a sample from my shopping list of items unavailable in community and most places in Cameroon:

1. Cheese
2. Mushrooms
3. Coffee (the real stuff, not the instant stuff that has the consistency and taste of used motor oil)
4. Peas
5. Aluminum foil
6. Yogurt
7. Butter
8. Seasonings

And don't even bother looking for peanut butter, sliced bread or a gallon of milk. The next time you visit the local supermarket, just take a few seconds to walk down any aisle and stare in awe at the variety and abundance of goods readily available to you. I can already sense the wave of "culture shock" rushing over me when I'm standing in the canned goods section. We forget what we can live without until we do it; we forget how much we really have until we lose it.

Many people ask me why it costs so much to live in a developing country. I won't give my thoughts on the use of the word "developing" here, but for now let me try to shed some light on the extraordinary cost of living in a place where the average person is making a few dollars a day. If we chose to live according to the standard of many of those around us, we would be living in a mud-brick house with a thatched roof, eat rice and beans on a regular basis, raise a good deal of our own food (or food to sell at the market) and abandon any form of insurance or personal transportation. However, that's not a realistic scenario nor does it leave any room for doing the other work we have come to do. Even if we did choose to live under these conditions, we would still have to pay for things like renewed Visas and host country taxes.

The reality is that we live on the upper echelon of the ladder in the Cameroonian community, and I am not saying this in a sarcastic or condescending way. Although our living conditions would be considered substandard in America, they are far above the standard where we live in Cameroon. We have such luxuries as plumbing, a gas stove and refrigerator and a hot water heater. Our windows and doors are secured, and there are only a handful of spiders, cockroaches and scorpions that frequent our house (often on the shower curtain unfortunately). We have a metal roof, a concrete floor and electricity when the generators in town are operational. If these don't sound like "luxuries" to you, then you need to seriously consider stepping beyond the frontiers of the United States and spend a respectable amount of time in a developing country. And I'm not referring to a tourist destination that is a small oasis of consumerism among a desert of poverty. Venture out a little further just beyond the Westernized shops and hotels to the reality behind the mirage of money.

The economic term "supply and demand" is in full effect here. Fuel is about $5 a gallon compared to approximately $3 in the States, a box of cereal is pushing $9 and don't even ask what it costs to purchase or import a reliable vehicle. The same goes for many building materials. On the other hand, labor is cheap as well as many simple electronic items that are imported from countries like Nigeria or China. Clothing, if made from locally available materials by a local tailor, is quite reasonable, not to mention colorful and comfortable. Hand-crafted furniture and locally-grown foods aren't too hard on the budget either. When it comes to appliances, tools or more sophisticated electronics, though, forget it.

I've been amazed again and again by what you can actually find if you look hard enough. The challenge is locating the item and then negotiating the price. Cameroonian stores tend to be a conglomeration of mismatched items. Inventories change frequently as do the prices. Imagine walking into the local hardware store and haggling over the price of a handful of nails (nothing comes in neat packages here). It makes for a very dynamic shopping experience that is both entertaining and potentially frustrating at the same time.

Cameroonians are also ingenious people when it comes to stretching what resources are available to them. For example, the technicians on the water team often lack fittings to put pieces of pipe together, like couplings and adapters. Their solution is to heat the pipe over an open fire until it is flexible enough to fit over the other piece. Even the children will make toys out of the most obscure items, like an abandoned bicycle rim that can be pushed down the road with a stick or an old sardine can fashioned into a car. And how the taxi drivers manage to keep their vehicles running considering the mechanical state of most of them is still a mystery to me…

MARCH 1, 2008

What follows is an account of events the past week during a nation-wide strike in Cameroon and my efforts to get home amidst the chaos. I was only able to send out one short e-mail correspondence during this time, so this will bring you up to speed on what took place both before and after that time. I want to thank all of you for your prayers during this period of uncertainty. God's hand was evident all along the way as he continued to put the right people and transport in my path that eventually brought me back safely (although quite stinky and dirty) to my wife yesterday evening.

Wednesday, February 20th:
I was awakened this morning on my thirty-first birthday by the sound of a rooster crowing. This may not seem unusual except for the fact it was actually in the house where I and ten other men are sleeping during the installation of a hand dug well in a refugee village. This will be our place of residence for the next three weeks or so while we attempt to dig a well approximately 60 feet into the soils of eastern Cameroon. The house we have rented for only $12 USD is actually in the neighboring village within walking distance to the well site. It is normally vacant and belongs to the *jarro's*, or chief's, son. It is the only home with a metal (or zinc as they call it) roof and concrete floor. Nine of the workers sleep in the main room on makeshift beds of foam while the supervisor and I have been provided the two rooms in the house.

I have received the "master bedroom", as there is a built-in latrine attached to it. Essentially it is a hand dug pit covered with a concrete slab. I can't help but think of that thin slab collapsing beneath me every time I stand on it. There is a small 3-inch hole for certain activities located in the center. I'll let you use your imagination here. It would probably be more accurate to call this area the cockroach breeding room. Every evening I am greeted by the dozens of six-legged roommates that emerge from their abode. It makes my evening bucket shower an interesting experience to say the least. My mosquito net is usually adequate to keep my bed private, but unfortunately this is not always the case. By the way, waking up with a cockroach on your face is not a pleasant experience.

The water situation has become quite desperate here as the dry season pushes on and their limited supply of water seeping from the hillside has begun to dry up. The water that remains is nothing more than two stagnant polls of tainted water, which appears to be contributing to a number of digestive ailments. We are encouraging them to boil all their drinking water, but it is not a practice to which they are accustomed. An influx of approximately 50 more refugees from the Central African Republic has exacerbated the situation. Highway robbers and bandits, the product of civil unrest and political instability in this neighboring country, continue to raid innocent Fulbe families who are forced across the border with the one thing they have left – their lives. The existing population in the village is doing what they can to accommodate these new residents by providing shelter and what little food is available. Our involvement with the village has enabled us to bring additional resources through the contributions of several organizations and individuals.

As I consider the circumstances of this particular event in my life, I praise God in the acknowledgement of prayers answered both for the refuges and for myself. They have been earnestly praying for aid to meet their growing physical needs, and we have been fervently praying for an opportunity to share the Good News with the Fulbe in both word and deed. It is humbling and overwhelming to consider all the events and decisions that have brought us here to this particular moment at this particular time and this particular people to fulfill what we have all been called to do as followers of Christ – to reach the unreached.

Saturday, February 23rd:

This entry comes to you after savoring a meal comprised of chicken and corn fufu, which I described previously. Chicken is one of those food items that has become a real treat. Preparing it is not a simple matter of opening the package and throwing it on the grill or purchasing a nicely seasoned, pre-cooked rotisserie chicken at the supermarket. It's much more complicated than that here. It begins with the usual negotiation at the open air market. However, in this case you are bargaining for a live animal. Of course the purchase of a live animal also means you must kill it, pluck it, clean it and butcher it before even considering throwing it in the 'ol frying pan. Needless to say, chicken had not been our dinner table much since we've arrived.

Today, however, it a special day; after five days of digging we have finally reached the water table about 15 meters below the ground, or approximately 50 feet for the metric-challenged like me. Try to imagine looking into this 5-foot diameter hole and seeing two men at the bottom laboriously and fearlessly chipping away at sand and gravel. I'm looking at in now and have a hard time believing I have allowed men to enter this abyss. Such is the way it is done in many counties throughout the world. These men are well experienced and show no fear in this subterranean environment. Perhaps the real scary part is that we still have another 4+ meters to go into the more treacherous aquifer material when we try to sink the water intake structure. For that stage of the work we will employ a double diaphragm, pneumatically-operated pump to remove water from the hole while simultaneously pumping air to the workers.

The discovery of the water table is a cause for celebration and traditionally accompanied by this meal to provide strength and encouragement for the work ahead while acknowledging the work completed. We are only about one-third of the way through the well installation. The next step will consist of construction of inner and outer concrete block walls. The outer wall extends from the water table to the surface while the inner wall will serve as the water intake and be dug down a minimum of 4 meters into the water to avoid the potential for it to dry up during the dry season, as is often the case here.

We have already observed many wells in this part of the country that are no longer producing water because of inadequate well depth. It will be several months before the water table begins to rise again. Most people in the area retrieve their water from small streams or seepage from the hillside. The water quality is extremely poor and appears to cause a significant amount of illness. The connection between contaminated water and sickness is still a foreign concept to many. Consequently, many people blame their symptoms on more familiar diseases like malaria. It is our hope that this new well will alleviate at least some of the physical suffering experienced by the refugees and build a bridge to ease their spiritual suffering as well.

Sunday, February 24th:

I can now officially say I have travelled by bush plane, train and automobile (and motorcycle) in Cameroon following my first train ride. You know those movies where people are frantically trying to get out of town because the aliens or monsters have arrived? That is sort of what it's like boarding the train in Cameroon. Perhaps it would be more accurately compared to a no holds barred wrestling match. All I remember during boarding is desperately grasping whatever was available as I was pushed through the doorway. Bags, children and shouts passed by, on, over and under me. The situation didn't improve once inside the railway coach. I soon learned I had made several serious blunders. The first was the purchase of a second class ticket. The second was the decision to pay the extra money for the *place entière*, or full seat, versus the *demi-place*, or half a seat. I soon discovered there was absolutely no difference between the two because there were no assigned seats, and it was every man, woman and child for themselves (at least there were no animals to compete with, too).

After aimlessly wandering the crowded aisles several times, a Fulbe man in his thirties finally offered me a smile and seat across from him that had been made to look occupied by a few carefully arranged belongings. Suleymanu, as the man had introduced himself, was on his way to the commercial capitol of Doula to find work. He spoke rather fluent English, which he had learned by watching TV and hosting American Peace Corps volunteers at his home. Suleymanu's desire was to become a radiologist and travel to remote villages and hospitals to help the poor with mobile equipment. As is often the case here, the passion was there but the money and means were not. Suleymanu had sat in second class because he thought that perhaps he would have the opportunity to interact with the poor. He found it rather humorous that he ended up sitting next to an American and my traveling companion, a Cameroonian "big man" as they call those of important stature.

The voyage was an overnight trip that began at 9 p.m. and was anticipated to arrive in Yaoundé, the capitol, at 8 a.m. the next morning. I had hoped things would quiet down a bit once the trip began, but to my dismay the level of activity only increased. Vendors emerged from nowhere with their well-rehearsed sales pitch and latest products. These consisted of numerous drugs, ink pens and bonbons, or candy. Several heated debates began regarding topics such as media bias and how old children should be to travel alone. This continued until nearly 3 a.m.

We arrived at our destination only to discover there was a taxi strike. In a city that depended almost exclusively on taxi transport for the average citizen, this was no small matter. The strike was in response to the cost of fuel in the country and was actually occurring simultaneously in many other metropolitan areas. After some discussion about the situation with my traveling companion, he indicated that most people lack a concept of a global market where fuel prices are impacted by many factors. However, the price of fuel in Cameroon did not fluctuate; it was ever-increasing according to him.

The scenario was further complicated by the fact protests were happening across the country in a response to a proposed constitutional amendment. The most significant outcry to this change occurred in Doula where two people were killed in the protests. Numerous fires had been lit in the streets, and all traffic had stopped due to roadblocks across the city. They were the product of angry protestors and youth. In Yaoundé, where we had arrived, the situation was not as desperate. Those with private vehicles were still able to travel freely throughout the city, but the average citizen was forced to walk to their destination, if possible. Many businesses were closed, and the markets were much quieter than usual.

It was obvious our timing for this particular trip was less than ideal. Our intent had been to come in search of materials to prepare for the installation of a drilled well in April. In the U.S., these materials are readily available. In Cameroon, however, finding well screen, drilling mud, etc. is quite the challenge. Drilled wells are rare, and the materials to install them are even rarer. Besides the special pipe and materials, the sand for the filter pack around the well will have to be created using locally-available sand and a series of experiments. The materials will most likely come from Doula, but the prospects of making a trip there are not good given the current state of unrest.

Monday, February 25:
Our trip to Yaoundé was involuntarily extended today following the cancellation of our train back to northern Cameroon. Escalation of the civil unrest in Doula had led to fears that those who are striking against the elevated fuel costs may also feel compelled to lash out against other forms of transportation, like the railway. We made it as far as boarding the train last night when they informed us 30 minutes later it was cancelled. Although we were told to keep our tickets and they would be honored the following day, there was no guarantee of this.

The cancellation of the train was not a major surprise after following the day's events in Doula, where more people had been killed in the protests and the city was paralyzed by roadblocks, protests and no taxi activity. It is difficult to distinguish whether the conflict is a product of the disgruntled taxi drivers, the protesting citizens or both. We are hearing reports from around the country that similar things are happening elsewhere in the urban areas. I am beginning to understand how quickly things can take a turn for the worse in an African country. On one hand, I am impressed with how quickly a group of people, like the taxi drivers, were able to unite under a common cause and carry through with a cohesive plan and single voice. On the other hand, I am appalled with how quickly people will resort to violence, vandalism and riots to resolve their problems. Numerous buildings and public property were destroyed. The underlying and omnipresent poverty is a dangerous catalyst coupled with a strong desire for political change.

I witnessed the eruptive nature surrounding these circumstances first-hand today while passing some time in an internet café. In the middle of communicating some of these events electronically in an e-mail, I suddenly found myself overwhelmed by what I thought were truck fumes entering the building. My eyes began to water and I found it somewhat difficult to breath. If you saw the exhaust from some of the trucks here, you would understand why I mistook this for fumes! What I erroneously thought was truck exhaust was actually the remnants of tear gas that had made its way into the internet café. Apparently a group of taxi drivers had attacked a motorcycle taxi that had ignored the strike and was carrying passengers anyways. As all of this was taking place, the business owner nonchalantly closed the main doors and carried on with business as usual. I find the resilience of Cameroonians to such extraordinary events admirable and frightening at the same time. It seems my reaction to many things I witness here is a series of conflicting emotions.

I can't help but wonder if all of this was making the American or international news. In my African world, nothing could be more important. But as an American, I know such events are likely not significant enough to make the evening news. We tend to work in numbers when it comes to news stories – 50,000 refugees, 80 dead, millions displaced. It's easy to be disconnected from a number. Civil unrest in African countries is accepted as the norm, and it doesn't catch our attention until we can no longer ignore it or are directly impacted. Those numbers have now taken a face for me, and it is now my reality, not just an image on the TV screen. I can't help but to reflect on how much we as Americans see but don't hear, hear but don't know, know but don't care.

Tuesday, February 26:

One of the many things I lost in America that I have found in Cameroon is time. Many hours pass waiting for transportation or in transit. Time loses its meaning and value here. I am left with much of it to reflect on events and write down my thoughts. We don't realize how much time enslaves us in America, both physically and mentally. We are consumed by appointments, meetings, schedules and the like. We use time and speed-oriented phrases like "the rat race", or "beat the clock" or "race against time". My greatest pet peeve in America had been those who don't "respect the clock". I find the concept almost humorous now.

I am currently "passing the time" in the Yaoundé train station. We arrived at 2:00 p.m. hoping to discover if the train would be cancelled again this evening. The station employee kindly directed us to pray about the matter. This had already been done several times, so we continued with the current course of action – spend the next four hours waiting for the scheduled departure and God's response. It came about five hours later when we were informed the train would not depart until 3 a.m. The reason for this was not provided, but I suspected that is was for the safety of the passengers. It was probably less likely that angry mobs would strike at 3 a.m. than 6 p.m. This means we have eight more hours of waiting followed by 12 hours of travel, assuming, of course, nothing else changes. Welcome to travel in Africa…

Wednesday, February 27:
One day and several hundred kilometers later. I now find myself in the town of Bafoussam. Our situation in Yaoundé did not improve yesterday as the strike continued and conditions worsened throughout the country. We spent the night in the crowded train station on makeshift beds of luggage and benches, if you could find one, awaiting our delayed departure time of 3 a.m. An announcement at 3:30 a.m. provided some hope that we would actually board the train as anticipated. After two hours of standing in line, it became painfully obvious this was not the case. The crowd began to become hostile as tired passengers began to lash out at the workers on the other side of the locked gate as well as each other. The man next to me yelled out in French, "We are not refugees! We are not foreigners! We are Cameroonians! This is not normal!" This sparked a chain reaction of arguments fueled by fatigue and uncertainty.

An hour later the gate opened and there was a mad rush of passengers to the train. The hurried efforts were futile, however, as the train maintained its stationary position for 1 hour, then 2 and then 3. A passenger announced a rumor that the train would not depart until its normally scheduled time of 6 p.m. that evening. From the train, we were able to observe the movement of taxis on the road again. Thinking the strike had ended, we decided to pursue a different course of action. We requested reimbursement at the ticket window and ventured out of the station to find a taxi to long-distance public transport.

Once we were touring the streets of the capitol in the taxi, we realized the strike was not officially over. Our driver nervously maneuvered the city streets and asked us to roll up our windows in fear striking drivers would throw objects at his car, and, even worse, his passengers. He explained that he had decided to return to work that morning after seeing several taxi drivers back on the job. Apparently there was no single voice orchestrating these activities. There was a palpable tension throughout the city as we worked our way towards the bush taxi park. We found a flurry of activity at a park on the north side of town where drivers were attempting to fill their taxis. Men came out of the crowd and began pulling on our arms and bags in an effort to guide us to their own vehicles. We squeezed into a taxi like a couple of sardines and were quickly on the road, which is quite rare.

I felt a bit uneasy when I realized we were the only vehicles on the road in either direction. The trip was going well until we encountered some barrels in the road with palm fronds sticking out of them. This was apparently a signal not to continue further, and we pulled into a *gendarmerie* (i.e. police station) where several other bush taxis were seeking refuge with their 20 or so passengers. The local merchants quickly took advantage of the potential for so many clients. The water and unidentifiable bush meat they brought disappeared as quickly as it had arrived. I passed on the bush meat, by the way. Our period of waiting had begun once again.

An hour or two later, passengers began to board their respective taxis again. Once inside ours, a request was made by the driver to collect 500 cfa (or about $1 USD) from each passenger to assist in paying the bribes he anticipated as we continued our trek to Bafoussam. Our driver's prediction came true as we reached the outskirts of the city. We were initially greeted by several burned vehicles and debris scattered in the roadway. Eventually we reached a manned roadblock commanded by dozens of youth. Their ages ranged from early teens to early twenties. Several of them wielded a bottle or cup of palm wine, a local fermented beverage that I was certain would not improve our situation.

The youth approached our small convoy like a swarm of angry African bees. They demanded we tell them where we got the *carburant* (i.e. fuel) while shouting about liberty. My fears that the presence of a white man would exacerbate and change the dynamics of the situation were confirmed when one of them identified me. I was immediately considered one of the factors in their elevated fuel costs. From what I gathered, they believed I was an oil company employee and a seed of exploitation. After explaining who I was and why I was in the country, the precarious crowd next to our vehicle calmed down. The individual I assume was their leader approached me and asked, "You have liberty in your country, don't you?" I agreed but tried to explain we do not seek it this way knowing, though, that my own inalienable rights that I often take for granted did not come about through peaceful negotiations.

Our drivers continued to negotiate our passage as we patiently awaited the outcome. An approaching motorcycle taxi had taken some of the attention off of us as they harassed this man and his passenger. They eventually confiscated his motorcycle and road off with it. The new passenger took a long chug from his bottle of palm wine and behaved like unrestrained youths do when there is no authority to control them. I wondered where the multitude of police officers had gone. Under normal circumstances, they were unavoidable. Now, there was not a single one to be found for hundreds of kilometers. They probably feared the response of so many belligerent youth to a uniformed officer.

As I awaited the verdict from the driver, a wave of emotions overtook me as I pondered our predicament. I felt angry to be treated in such a way by the people I had come to help. I felt pity for so many unemployed, hungry youth who were simply taking advantage of an opportunity to put some money in their pockets to survive. I felt ashamed to be an American with so many rights, opportunities and material wealth while so many suffered in this world. These boys had found a chance to express their frustration, a cause to unite under. The reality was they probably felt they had nothing better to do and nothing to lose.

The driver finally returned successfully from his negotiations. For a few dollars, we had escaped a potentially dangerous situation. This was only the beginning of a series of similar negotiations and hostile crowds. A few thousand francs were like kryptonite to these youth. Judging from the number of burnt vehicles on the road, I believe we would have found ourselves in a much more serious situation a day or two earlier when the strike had begun.

We arrived at the taxi park in Bafoussam to the sound of cheers from those who thought they had lost 3 vehicles in their fleet. The town was an eerie contrast to the bustling African streets I had passed through 2 weeks earlier. Although people walked the streets, businesses were closed and there was an uncomfortable silence that was not Cameroonian. Occasionally I would be hailed by a group of youth who praised me in sharing in their suffering by walking on foot. Of course I had no choice, but I wasn't about to tell them that. At other times I would be asked if I were a Frenchman through angry stares. Many of the Cameroonian woes were also being blamed on the French, who some claimed were continuing to exploit their resources and people. The ghost of colonialism haunts the minds of many. Its effects are difficult to measure, but it's evident that it hinders progress and relationships.

Our trek on foot eventually brought us to the Bafoussam Baptist Health Center, a safe refuge for now. We were greeted by the center director and joined with another group of Cameroonians who had found themselves in a similar situation after completing some community health work in a nearby village. A short walk took us to a local hotel where they were staying. Five thousand francs, or about $10, bought a room with a bed and working lights. They considered the price far too high, but, after spending two nights at the train station, I was willing to pay a lot more for a good night's rest. I was reinvigorated by a meal of fried chicken and real french fries, the first I had eaten since arriving in the country.

I was uncomfortably awakened at 1:35 a.m. by my digestive system followed by a subsequent trip to the bathroom. It appeared that Cameroonian fried chicken did not agree as well with me as American fried chicken. I suppose there were several African practices that weren't agreeing with me these days.

Thursday, February 28:

Another day has passed in Bafoussam with little change in the state of the country. I would dare to say that things have even worsened slightly following a 5-minute address by the president yesterday evening. During his speech, the president's response to the current crisis was the deployment of whatever lawful means were necessary to maintain peace in Cameroon. In other words, according to my hotel companions, the military would be given free reign to quench the violence however they saw fit.

That is exactly what happened this morning as we heard a report that a convoy of approximately fifteen military vehicles had passed our hotel earlier headed into town. Gunshots were heard later, but it was not certain where the final destination of the bullets may have been. Reports streamed across the shortwave radio about continued protests, violence, vandalism and deaths. It appeared the president's words had only fueled the fire of protest. Businesses remained closed, taxis were parked and youth continued their tire burning and debauchery.

We passed most of the day at the health center discussing the state of the country, the president's speech and solutions to the current crisis. I was surprised by the unity I witnessed in the discussions I heard. People did not appear to be divided in their interpretation of the situation at hand, the causes or the solutions. Behind all of it was a strong desire for political change. Everyone had felt the strain of corruption, increased fuel and commodity prices and limited employment opportunities. They did not agree with the response of the youth, but they understood their frustration. They believed the strike was necessary but violence was not.

I was further amazed that there were no individual leaders emerging as the voices behind the activities. It was truly a unified effort formed by the people and for the people. It was not a voice driven by selfish political ambitions but rather a voice driven by a desire for a better life. With such unity and oneness of purpose, I began to fear there may not be a simple or short solution on the horizon.

Friday, February 29:

My week-long journey and this national strike have nearly come to an end. I find myself in the back of a bush taxi on its way to Banyo, my Cameroonian home. It's a 6 to 8 hour journey I look forward to after sleepless nights in train stations and uncomfortable beds. I almost welcome the flood of dust that is currently filling my nostrils as I try to scratch down my thoughts on bumpy roads.

Much to everyone's relief, most things have returned to normal after a multiple day strike over the rising prices of fuel and commodities, constitutional changes and taxation. Many have told me it would have ended sooner if the president's address to the nation would have brought hope instead of rebuke, solutions rather than force.

There are rumors that trouble persists in many of the Anglophone cities, where it is said by some that oppression is felt most due to francophone domination. My own experience has not supported this view, as I have seen many Anglophone regions significantly more developed than the Francophone Province where I currently reside.

My gut feeling is that all this is simply the calm before the storm. Our bush taxi just stopped to fuel up, and gas prices have dropped from 594 cfa/liter to 583 cfa/liter. Although this is not significant in terms of an actual cost savings to the consumer, where this represents a drop of about $0.02, it is a significant response for citizens who have not seen a decrease in fuel prices for a long time. I asked the station attendant if people were happy with the drop in price. He responded without hesitation, "No," and indicated the strike would probably continue. I was told the last time something like this occurred, it lasted for 3 months with some commercial activity on the weekends. Time will tell what the future holds.

I will tell you what I do know – God is in control and we are not. This six-day "excursion" has been one of those faith-building moments where God's providence in my life is reaffirmed in a new way. Sometimes things need to be totally out of our hands before we acknowledge just how dependent we are on God's grace, love and mercy. Spiritual transformation is an on-going process and occurs over the course of the events in our life.

I can't say I've ever had quite an experience like this one where one minute I had a defined program humming right along and the next thing I know there is complete chaos with no answers and lots of questions. Even when 9/11 happened I didn't feel as impacted or touched as I did with this event that had upset my plans directly and very negatively, or so I thought.

I look back at the chain of events that have now brought me back safely to my wife and African home, and I see God's hand at work from the night we found transport from the train station after being stranded without taxis, to the availability of a room in Yaoundé, to the brave and wise driver who brought us safely through hostile territory, to the fellow brothers in Christ who were stranded with us in Bafoussam and cared for us during our stay there, to the opening of a safe passage to Banyo on the last taxi out of town where I now find myself writing you. There is no doubt my faith has taken another step forward on this journey and He has molded me a little more. It is always difficult to express on the outside what is happening inside. I hope the last several journal entries have brought you along vicariously and maybe even molded you a little.

Saturday, March 1:

As if to provide a final confirmation of God's hand in my recent experience, I will just mention I recently received a call from Suleymanu, the man we met the first night on the train to Yaoundé. He is still stranded at the train station…

MARCH 4, 2008

The rains have finally arrived, and with them come a sense of renewal. The veil of dust that has hidden life from our eyes has now been lifted to reveal the lush greenness of the landscape again. The gentle tapping on our metal roof is soothing to the ears. Everyone is busy preparing their farms, including us. The small plot of land behind our house has become a terraced garden of refuge where I sometimes go to gather my thoughts or simply to have none at all. Some people may mistake my garden for the local prison with its foreboding barbed wire and impenetrable chicken wire. I have now long waged war against the *mbewa*, or goat. Now that the rains have arrived, there are many more delicacies to tantalize their insatiable appetite. The locals probably find it humorous that I even attempted to plant anything before the rains. My wimpy-looking watermelon and squash only add to their argument.

There's a peace in working the land I discovered while trying my hand at small-scale farming in the U.S. during our stay at a small farm in Florida. I find the same peace here when in need of physical refuge in the midst of cultural or spiritual turmoil. I guess I have a similar peace in writing down my thoughts and experiences as I am now. The sense of connecting to a world so far away from our own right now is comforting even if these words only find themselves confined to these pages never to reach the eyes or minds of people who need to hear about the state of the world beyond their own.

In a country where things tend to move at a much slower pace than that to which we are accustomed, I still can't seem to find enough time. Perhaps it represents poor acclimation on my part to our new environment. Perhaps it's the sense of overwhelming needs here that sometimes overtakes me like an ocean wave. The needs in our small community alone can make your efforts feel inadequate. Now that the local community has become used to our presence, we find many more people at our door seeking assistance to mostly physical needs. We have tried to use a great deal of discretion in determining who we help, but learning to say "no" is surely one of the hardest things we have to do here.

It is far too easy to feel as if you're not doing enough in this place. It's a very dangerous emotion, though, that will quickly lead to frustration and a sense of being burned out. It is not Biblical to respond in such a way. We know as Christians we cannot work our way into heaven, but at the same time we know we were created for good works.[1] It's a daunting task to find where these ideas come into equilibrium. I remember some advice given to us regarding this matter. We were told we can be worn out by doing things <u>in</u> His name versus the renewing power of doing it <u>for</u> His name as an act of worship and not an act of works. Being here now in this position, I get it. Boy, do I get it!

I consider our current circumstances here and see how we have been blessed in so many ways. Thanks to my predecessor, we inherited many things that would normally consume a great deal of a new arrival's time. For example, we didn't have to worry about finding a vehicle, building a house or establishing our respective ministries. This was provided to us with the opportunity to jump right in the ministry work. I have found my role here is more of a project manager, or facilitator, in many ways, and it has suited me well. My experience in the States has prepared me for managing the existing Cameroonian teams and subcontractors involved with the ministry projects.

However, I find at the same time I have also inherited many of the difficulties that have developed over time. Addressing the accumulated challenges of the past leads to great frustration and disappointment if we mistakenly apply human expectations. Paul said in Romans that he did not want to build on another man's foundation, and now I understand why.[2] I have intentionally tried not to ask too many questions about the past because I believe it would hinder my ability to hear how God was leading me in this ministry. I know He has brought me to this particular place at this particular time to help fulfill His purpose of bringing the Gospel as a testimony to all the nations.[3]

At times I think it would have been easier to start from my own foundation, but I don't believe that is His plan for my involvement in Cameroon. God knows my gifts and weaknesses, both which glorify Him. We are His creation. Again I am reminded of Paul's words in 2 Corinthians[4] where the Lord said to Him, "My grace is sufficient for you, for my power is made perfect in weakness." Never before have my weaknesses been so exposed, and never before has the Lord seemed more powerful.

REFLECTIONS ON TRANSFORMATION

Transformation is at the heart of everything my wife and I are hoping to achieve as we continue on this journey. Perhaps one of the greatest revelations in my life is that unless a change in the physical condition of an individual is accompanied by a change in the spiritual condition, then true transformation has not occurred; minds and hearts must be renewed to create a lasting change in people. When our hearts are transformed, so are our actions. And when our actions are transformed, so is the world.

It is not enough just to improve the physical state of an individual or community. Sometimes such a one-sided approach only results in equipping people with the tools and resources to worsen their condition; essentially a sinner is enabled to sin better. If we take a holistic approach to meeting needs where physical, social and spiritual components of life are addressed simultaneously, then true transformation is possible. A sincere, genuine love in Christ for people transcends cultural boundaries, language barriers and the like.

In order to be in the world but not of the world, we must be transformed. This requires that we abandon the mold established by this world and are renewed beginning from within. We know we are to no longer to conform to the pattern established by the lusts and temptations of the world as we seek transformation of the mind. From the moment we leave the womb, we are confronted by this pattern. There are expectations established for our development that are shaped by our respective cultures and environments. From the clothes we wear to the words we say to the thoughts we think, these elements begin to create our character and define our reason for being. These forces begin to push and squeeze us into the mold that may or may not conform to God's will. If it does not, we must break free and live with renewed minds and purpose.

Living for God does not mean we abandon all goals, comforts and pleasures; living for Him means our goals, comforts and pleasures fall in line with His will for our lives. They take on different meaning and are transformed from something recognized by the world to something not recognized by the world. When we abandon the desires of the flesh and make the things of this world subject to us rather than us being subject to them, we can better discern God's will and distinguish it from our own.

Although surrendering to God's plan can often be difficult, especially in the face of suffering and persecution, sometimes the greater challenge is discerning God's will. The first step in identifying God's plan is to recognize the world's pattern; the world lacks a God-centered view, and, therefore, is self-centered. The world's thoughts and actions are guided by selfish desires to please itself rather than God. When we recognize those things that please God, we may begin to break the pattern of world conformity and self-centeredness. We must reflect on and pursue those things that are noble, right, pure, lovely, admirable, excellent and praiseworthy, as the apostle Paul reminds us.[5]

I sense a great deal of transformation occurring in my own life as we continue to explore our roles in Cameroon and this world. There are new trials that would be difficult to fathom back home, and they challenge our faith and commitment to what we have begun. What type of people will we be when this first year in Africa comes to an end? How will our direction in life have been altered? How will we have been transformed?

REFLECTIONS ON FAITH

As we continue on this journey, my understanding of trusting in God completely continues to grow with each new test of faith. The rubber has hit the proverbial road, and I have reached a better awareness of what God demands of us – everything. He doesn't want part of me; He wants all of me. This includes my time, energy and talents, which are gifts from Him to be used to glorify Him.

As is often the case, though, saying something and living it are two entirely different matters. It seems there is always something to hold back, and, by doing so, we deprive ourselves of the opportunity to truly understand what it means to completely put our trust in God. Getting on that plane to head to Africa was a major crossroad in my life. It was by no means a casual commitment. I knew the comforts and pleasures I was leaving behind (from a material standpoint at least) and only had a vague idea of what awaited me in Cameroon.

One thing that followed me from America, though, was fear – fear of failure, fear of the future and fear of finances. Fear is not of God[6], and this continues to be a difficult obstacle in my efforts to fully trust God for all my needs. Stepping out of our comfort zone is a very revealing process, and those things that we allowed to define us are exposed as they are taken away, such as our careers, possessions and relationships. Faith is that enduring quality that remains when all else has vanished. Living by faith is about overcoming our fears and handing everything over to God. For myself, the fear of failure that I carried with me from the States indicates 1) that I believe there is something I can do on my own to prevent failure, and 2) I am not trusting that God will use my failures as instruments of character building and spiritual maturation.

We must abandon those things that distract us from God and pursue those things which glorify Him. I am by no means suggesting that we abandon everything irresponsibly in such a way that we become a burden to others. It has been a long process of preparations and prayers to finally get to the point where we could leave for Africa. The logistical issues associated with going overseas for an extended period of time were quite overwhelming at times, and we questioned whether or not it was even going to be possible. But all things are possible with God[7], and doors opened along the way as we kept refocusing our time, energy and resources away from ourselves and towards God.

As an engineer, it would seem that I fall into an unusual category of science-minded people who have no problem reconciling their faith with science. I believe that someone had to make all those laws governing the universe, which are no less a part of creation than an animal or a plant or you and I. The deeper I dwell into the intricacies of that creation, the more I believe the evidence for an intelligent designer mounts. My profession has brought me into contact with many agnostics and atheists who have rationalized God away or find more comfort in intellect and reason than what I have often heard referred to as "blind faith". Many of these people are my closest friends, and many a debate (friendly debates, most of the time at least) have been had over these different worldviews. Now I find myself in a world where science remains relatively unknown and faith rules supreme. Where that faith lies varies dramatically, however, from person to person and people group to people group.

The Christian faith, however, is by no means blind. The historical, archeological and manuscript evidence in support of the doctrines that comprise the Christian faith are overwhelming compared to the evidence for other worldviews. As I said earlier, though, it is not my intent to be a theologian here or an apologist; I will leave that to much more qualified individuals. Therein, though, is the beauty of faith. It is not reserved for the elite or only well-educated; it is not only discovered by the poor or downtrodden. Faith is obtainable by all. It is faith that leads to action and action that leads to righteousness. We are reminded of this in the story of Abraham and Isaac, where Abraham's willingness to obey God by giving up his only son was "credited to him as righteousness" by his actions.[8] Likewise, our faith in this day and age should stir in us a call to action in response to the state of the world and the sin that has invaded it. Our society is being plagued by a disease that is consuming our souls as people turn outwardly to man instead of inwardly to God for answers to life's questions.

Christians often speak of a "calling" in their lives. I would say that we have been called to serve in Africa and have ventured out on faith. No, there was no booming voice in the sky accompanied by a brilliant light or any supernatural event that led us to that decision. However, there is a lifetime of events that have led us in this direction that I believe bares the hand of God. I don't want this to be a biography, so I won't go into those kinds of details. I would just recommend that you look at your own life and see where perhaps God has opened doors to you.

It is not uncommon for people to lavish us with praise when we tell them about what we're doing. Often people will say, "I've always wanted to do that", or "I could never do that." We by no means consider ourselves worthy of this task of declaring the Gospel where it is unknown in word and deed, but we also don't consider what we're doing out of reach for each and every one of us who makes a commitment to serve God in whatever capacity or form that may take. My hope is that we can be an example to those that consider themselves "average individuals" in our society to step out and seek the change and be the change the world desires.

Trusting in God has taken on new meaning as my wife and I have transitioned into this phase of our lives. In making this move, I have left my job in the consulting world and abandoned the financial security and sense of identity that I tend to associate with my career. I have ascended one step higher in seeking my identity in Christ. We are no longer investing in our 401k plans but instead are investing in our relationship with God, with others and with the world beyond our own. Nothing we can acquire in our careers, successes or investments will replace what we gain through these relationships. Our faith is being put to the test as we put the false idols of the world behind us and actively pursue a path that glorifies God in our daily living.

We must trust that every challenge or choice we face in this journey finds its answer in the Word of God. The more familiar we are with Scripture, the more prepared we are to face life head on. It is a living Word with power and all the authority it possessed when it was revealed to the men who served as God's chosen instruments to share it at the proper time. It is not a series of incoherent stories but instead is a cohesive story of

God's plan, purpose and promise. We learn of our origin, our purpose and destiny from this one source. It is an incredible gift that offers just a glimpse into the thoughts and ways of God.

The universal application of the Bible's truths and teachings is a strong witness to the authority it has in our lives. It has transcended boundaries of time, culture and geography in the face of great opposition and stands firmly grounded in historical truth. It remains a tangible testimony of God's plan and how we fit into that plan as beings created in His image. Until we accept its authority in our lives and embrace its truths, we cannot come to fully understand God's will for our lives. He has given us His very Word, both in writing and in the flesh, so that we may more fully understand who He is and who we are and what humanity could be. It is the story of sin, judgment and redemption that was made complete in Jesus Christ. The final victory is won, sin stands defeated and eternity awaits those who seek it. Death no longer reigns over us when we accept the free gift of salvation through faith in the atoning and redemptive sacrifice of Jesus Christ.[9]

---

[1] For we are God's handiwork, created in Christ Jesus to do good works, which God prepared in advance for us to do. (Ephesians 2:10)

[2] It has always been my ambition to preach the gospel where Christ was not known, so that I would not be building on someone else's foundation. (Romans 15:20)

[3] Therefore go and make disciples of all the nations, baptizing them in the name of the Father and of the Son and of the Holy Spirit. (Matthew 28:19).

[4] 2 Corinthians 12:9

[5] Philippians 4:8

[6] There is no fear in love. But perfect love drives out fear, because fear has to do with punishment. (1 John 4:18)

[7] Jesus looked at them and said, "With human beings this is impossible, but with God all things are possible." (Matthew 19:26)

[8] Abram believed the Lord, and he credited it to him as righteousness. (Genesis 15:6)

[9] for all have sinned and fall short of the glory of God, and all are justified freely by his grace through the redemption that came by Jesus Christ. (Romans 3:23-24)

CHAPTER 3

OUT OF THE CULTURAL HONEYMOON AND INTO PERSEVERANCE

MARCH 18, 2008

Africa is truly a continent of contrasts when compared to the world from which we have ventured. It does not become clear how much our respective societies have wired us until we leave the mold of our cultural identity. After four months of living in Cameroon, many of these contrasts have become blatantly, sometimes painfully, obvious.

We have transitioned out of what is known as the "honeymoon phase". This is considered one of the stages of culture shock. During this phase, everything seems new and exciting, a breath of fresh cultural air. Then you begin questioning why some things are done the way they are when they can obviously be done better per your own culture's methodology. Core ideas and principles are challenged, and the longing for certain aspects of home weigh heavily on your heart (not to mention stomach). Frustration, confusion and ethnocentrism are some of the emotions that accompany this transition out of the second stage of culture shock, and I seem to have found myself in the middle of it.

Take, for example, growing old. In America, we tend to distance ourselves from it. Youth and beauty are highly valued, and many are willing to spend much of their earnings and energy in finding ways to look, feel and act younger. Respect for the elderly has become almost old-fashioned, and it is not uncommon to find many senior citizens living at an assisted living establishment where they are expected to pass the rest of their remaining days. Not so in Africa. The elderly are venerated. Their wisdom is cherished by the community, and they are cared for by their families when they find time has taken away the ability for them to manage on their own. And when death comes, it is up close and personal.

I had an experience last week that introduced me to African death in a way I would never experience in America. A 24 year-old man had died from hepatitis at the hospital. Tiffany had spent some time with him while serving as his nurse. He was an orphan and was only survived by a younger brother and some very distant relatives. Because he lacked the family network that would be typical here, his burial arrangements and financial burdens were taken on by the church and local community. They pooled their limited financial resources and purchased a small wooden coffin and prepared the body for burial.

The nature of his disease caused a massive build-up of fluids in the body and required that it be prepared quickly to prevent the risk of infecting others at the hospital. Because I was the only person in the community with access to a truck at the time, I was asked to carry the body in the bed of a Toyota Hilux to the local cemetery about 5 miles away. When I pulled up to the hospital entrance, the coffin was loaded into the truck accompanied by a frenzy of about a dozen other people who crammed in around the wooden casket and inside the cab. Those who were not fortunate enough to find a place in the truck were squeezed into the hospital van and would be expected to pay a small transport fee.

The ride to the funeral was nerve-racking. I could not help but imagine an encounter with one of the innumerable potholes in our path that would send our fragile cargo up in the air. The lid had not been secured, as this would incur additional and unnecessary costs. I seemed to be the only one concerned about such possibilities as everyone continued with unrelated conversations.

The youth were still digging the grave when we arrived at the burial ground. They were taking turns chopping away at the gravelly soils with a pick axe and African "hoes", short shovels with L-shaped handles typically used to cultivate their fields. Most of them were still dressed in their Sunday best after coming straight from the church service.

As the work continued, a slow, melodic crescendo emerged amongst a group of women who had gathered under a nearby tree. The song they sang spoke of not knowing if this day would be our last. Several songs followed as the youth continued their descent into the earth. Others gathered in small groups seeking shade from the heat of the day until at last the work was complete.

The cemetery land had been donated by the local traditional leader, and it was divided in two according to religious affiliation. We were surrounded by several freshly-dug graves on the Christian side of the cemetery. Across the way one could see the land designated for the Muslim deceased. I quietly pondered the fate of those who die without knowing Christ. The community we lived in consisted of about 15,000 such people. More than a hundred times that did not know Christ in the country. And more than a thousand times that number did not know Him in the world. The task of taking the Gospel to the nations seemed overwhelming at that moment. The cost for not doing so was even more overwhelming.

JUNE 3, 2008

Our most recent ministry projects involve the installation of two drilled wells. The projects have challenged me to once again re-evaluate our ministry philosophy and ask the question, "Why are we here, and what exactly are we doing?" Our ministry motto has been, and I'm sure will continue to be, "reaching the unreached one need at a time". There are plenty of quick and easy Biblical responses to these questions. We are here to glorify God, to spread the love of Christ and the Good News, to provide for the physical and spiritual needs of those who need it most, to further the Kingdom of God, etc. But these responses only scratch the surface of what these things look like in our present reality. This reality is comprised of things like limited resources and seemingly unlimited needs, joy and sorrow, poverty and pain, and life and death. It is difficult to wrap all of this into a neat and clean package and say, "This is our ministry philosophy and how we do things." When faced with the difficult question of where we commit our time, monies, etc., I have yet to find a simple answer.

The different ministry philosophies seem to fall on two ends of a spectrum. On one side we find the approach of targeting people groups strategically who have not heard the Gospel message. On the other side, we find an approach where as much is done as possible in any setting in the name of Christ as a demonstration of the Good News. I now find myself somewhere in the middle sitting on the proverbial ministry fence trying to develop a vision and strategy for moving forward. Being involved in a water ministry, or any other "felt needs" based ministry, seems to make this exceptionally difficult because of the nature of it. There are many who do similar work without any mention of Christ, and the need for clean water is overwhelming. Approximately one billion people lack access to clean water; many more than that lack access to the Gospel.

I am not a theologian, nor do I have any formal Bible training that would provide me with the credentials to tackle these difficult questions. I am an engineer gone missionary with a heart for those who are lacking the things we often take for granted – ready access to clean drinking water and the purifying spiritual water of the Gospel. Early on in my career as an engineer I was introduced to different engineering philosophies. These also seemed to fall on a spectrum between over-designed systems and under-designed systems. In between these two extremes was an equilibrium (we like that word in engineering) that maximized resources and minimized failure. That is where I like to be in that field, and I believe it is where I like to be in this one.

    Of course failure is not a word we use on the field like we would use in engineering. If a bridge collapses or a structure falls, it is obvious an engineering failure occurs. The difference with ministry is that we know God does not always want our own plans to succeed, and it is only when we commit our plans to Him that we will find success, although it may not resemble the thing we had sought initially. I have lived most of my life with a fear of this thing we call failure, and I thought it was something that motivated me and caused me to excel. On the contrary, it was something that actually enslaved me and prevented me from being who I truly am in Christ. It marked a self-reliance and pride that only separates us from our Creator. When we embrace what we view as failures instead as opportunities for spiritual maturity and renewal, we become more of who we were meant to be and less of whom we think we are.

JUNE 28, 2008

No matter how long I stay in Africa, I don't think I will ever get used to the amount and types of things I have seen people, especially the women and children, carry on their heads. In the States, this is not a phenomenon to which we are accustomed. I see Cameroonians carry loads on their cranium that would surely leave me in the hospital with some kind of neck or back injury. I often receive strange looks or muffled laughs when I struggle to carry a 3-gallon pail of water while the child next to me gracefully walks pass with the same load on his or her head smiling at my efforts. Of course I've tried to throw things like water pails and cement on my head, but I only end up soak and wet or dirty. I was once told that an African woman can carry up to 20% of her body weight on her head without burning any extra calories! Apparently their balance and stride make this possible.

My amazement doesn't end there, though. The African skill at hauling things also carries over to vehicular transportation. Nothing is off limits when it comes to a load. Just to give you an idea, here are a few of my favorite loads I've seen while in Cameroon:

- Although three people on a 125cc motorcycle taxi is not uncommon, I once saw five people squeezed on one. One of them was an infant stuck between the handlebars…

- Although chickens are allowed inside the bush taxis, goats are not (we're thankful for that). However, they can ride on top of the bush taxi, where they spend hours tied to a luggage rack.

- You don't see trailers here to carry cattle or horses, but you will see them crammed into the bed of a small pick-up truck. Last week I saw three full-grown cattle in the back of a Toyota Hilux.

- Reinforcing bar, or rebar, for concrete construction is commonly used here with the abundance of concrete structures. Of course it would be too costly to hire a truck to carry a bundle of rebar, so the alternative is to hire a motorcycle taxi to drag the 20-foot lengths across the road to its destination.

➤ Probably the best load I've seen so far is a motorcycle carrying…another motorcycle.

JULY 8, 2008

Things I've Learned While Serving in Africa…

- Cameroon is not the end but only the beginning of a long-term ministry to unreached peoples.

- I've learned much about myself, the world and what God is doing in both.

- I've learned how not be afraid of things like failure, finances or the future.

- I've learned what the Gospel looks like and not just what it sounds like.

- I've learned about God's will for our lives as bridge builders and Kingdom builders.

- I've learned disappointment, forgiveness and trust in much deeper ways.

- I can have nothing or everything and it does not change who I am.

- You can't escape corporate America, even in Africa.

- My strengths and weaknesses are greatest in a culture outside my own; they are exposed in such a way that they are glaringly evident.

- Passion and compassion are forces to be reckoned with.

- Expectations can be very dangerous and even fatal to the best intentions.

- Good intentions do not always have good results.

- Too much theology and too little Gospel can be very destructive.

- A sinner can be equipped to sin better if transformation is not the goal.

- Ministry philosophies are as varied as political views.

- Truth is very grey in a culture where corruption rules.

- Exposing and upholding the truth does not win many friends.

- Independence is a difficult thing to give up, and pride is perhaps the greatest single hindrance to serving God.

- If there is no ownership in a project by the community, there is no future for the project in the community.

- Coming from a goal-oriented society tends to take our eye off the goal.

- People, not projects, should be our goal.

- In a relational society, shaming someone can be far more severe than lying to someone or stealing from them.

- We can never fully let go of our own culture and never truly assimilate into the one we are in.

- People are NOT the same everywhere. We may all live and die, laugh and cry, but how we do these things can be dramatically different.

- Living by faith takes a lot more work than living without it.

- Be careful when you answer God's call because He doesn't hang up the phone.

JULY 11, 2008

There are many inspiring and courageous stories about men and women who made tremendous impacts in the world in the name of the Lord. They were often people of humble backgrounds or troubled pasts that had committed themselves to something more than themselves, and, in doing so, were able to achieve more than they could as individuals seeking their own desires or selfish pleasures.

I remember one such story about Cameron Townsend. Cameron served as a missionary to the Cakchiquel people of Guatemala. He distributed Bibles in Spanish, but was challenged one day by a Cakchiquel man who posed the question, "If your God is so great, why can't he speak my language?" The consequence of that question was Wycliffe Bible Translators, one of the world's largest missionary organizations.

The question this man had posed compelled me to start asking some similar questions. For example, "If our God is so great, why don't all people have access to clean water and sanitation?" Or, "If our God is so great, why don't all people have access to basic health care?" Or, "If our God is so great, why don't all people have access to a stable food source?" As Cameron Townsend demonstrated, our God IS that great; the problem lies in us.

I would venture to say what is lacking in many Christians that leave these questions unanswered is a sense of purpose in this earthly life. We have a clear picture of what is to come, and we joyfully carry the hope of eternity with us as our inheritance in the life to come. But what about now? What did Christ say about our current life, our current commitments and obligations, our purpose here and now? Scripture would suggest he had a lot to say and show about our conduct in this world as transformed beings in him. He spoke of the will of God's kingdom being done on earth as it is in heaven.[1] He spoke of feeding the hungry, quenching the thirst of those without water, clothing the naked, inviting in the stranger, and caring for the sick and imprisoned.[2] He spoke of losing this life to find it.[3] He spoke of being the body of Christ, its members, with different functions as part of the whole.[4]

The Gospel message is not just about what is to come, but what is. We are to take the picture of heaven that has been placed in our hearts and bring it to the present the best we can in a fallen world. If we only share a message of what is to be and not what is, then how can we achieve the type of world transformation that we all yearn and groan for in this day and age of global uncertainty and looming peril?

Great things can happen when individuals commit themselves to something greater than themselves with a sense of passion and compassion, purpose and direction. God has given us the blueprint; we have only to build this Kingdom with our hearts and will. World change is a possibility, and we should not abandon the present for the hope of the future. The hope of the future has already arrived and is living in us.

JULY 16, 2008

Soccer, or "football" as it's known here, is one sport I really never picked up on. Had I known the incredible passion the rest of the world shared for it, I would definitely had made more of an effort to learn the rules and even play a bit back home. Consequently, I now find myself in the awkward position of learning a new sport in my 30's that most people here have been playing it seems since they took their first steps as an infant. This is another one of those instances where cultural assimilation has brought me back to appearing like a child again.

I should back up and explain how I became involved with the community soccer team. I think it will shed some light on how things sometimes take place around here. One of my friends from the hospital had casually mentioned to me that our neighborhood was going to register with the community football league. That day he had been on his way to an informational meeting to find out the details for registering. He invited me along, but I politely declined knowing my acceptance of the offer would automatically qualify me for committing to something I knew absolutely nothing about.

The next day I ran into my friend again, who invited me to another meeting where they would be electing the team committee. In Cameroon, it seems everything must have a committee with elected officials regardless of the activity, duration or significance of the event. Soccer is no exception. I was told that if I attended the meeting, I most surely would be elected to a position. That was all I needed to hear to know I would be occupied around that time.

Unfortunately my lack of attendance did not prevent me from being elected to the football board. I was approached by a group of delegates who happily informed me I had been elected president of the community football team. Despite my best efforts to explain that in order to be elected to a position you must be present during the selection of the candidates, in the end I had no choice but to except the position that had been bestowed upon me. As I looked over their list of members, I realized it was perfectly acceptable to be on the board even if you weren't playing on the team. The doctor, for example, although full of energy at 70, probably wasn't going to be joining the team on the field. His official position, however, was "Supporter".

Further inspection of the rather long list of committee members began to shed some light on my "roles and responsibilities" as President. It was interesting to note that two other names had been written in the space for President. I asked about these other "presidents", and I was informed that I was their first selection and the others would only be approached if I refused. Because I had accepted, however, there would now be no need to talk to the other potential candidates.

I was not surprised to find that the conversation quickly changed to team financial matters after my acceptance was finalized. I was told of the estimated budget for the team and of how much other supporters had already provided. I asked how much the president was expected to contribute to the team, and I was given the response of "whatever was in my heart" (i.e. whatever might happen to be in my wallet).

I was told practice would be in an hour and they would be expecting me. I figured as the newly "elected" president, I should at least make a showing. I had been interested in learning the game, but I thought I would begin by practicing with the elementary kids who were still well above my playing level. Now I would find myself among seasoned football veterans about 10 years younger and 100 pounds lighter. Not exactly how I wanted to begin my football career.

I tried to arrive at what I had considered would be a little late to practice and still managed to be the first one there. Thinking I may have mistaken which field we were playing on, I returned only to find a few members of the team beginning the trek. About an hour later, we finally had enough players to start a match. To my dismay, we were picked to be the "skins", so the fat white guy stood out just a little bit. And then there's that little tattoo I have of a Celtic cross on my shoulder. Nobody asked me about it, but I can only imagine some of things they were thinking.

I probably need to describe the playing field to give you a better picture of the conditions. The "field" is actually an uneven hard clay terrain littered with gravel, holes and whatever else may have found its way there. The boundaries are roughly the grassy edge that surrounds the playing area, and the goal posts are constructed of makeshift materials. It all made for a rather risky playing environment. Things did not improve when the afternoon rain arrived and the game continued. If you have had the experience of driving on what we call "black ice" in the northern states, hard clay becomes what I call "brown ice" when it's wet. We might as well have turned the ball into a puck and started playing hockey. After an hour and a half of being danced around and looking silly at my attempts to use my feet for something that was completely foreign to them, the match finally ended and I returned home to find what pride I had left.

Perhaps my role as president will be a less physical and more supportive in nature…

REFLECTIONS ON PERSEVERANCE

    Some days are certainly harder than others when you're so far from home and loved ones. Although we have found a new home and community in Africa, there are days when the cultural blues can really get you down. The support network you once reached out to is no longer there. It seems relationships develop quickly, though, in new environments. It's a lot like going to summer camp as a kid and finding a best friend you only knew for two weeks. We've been blessed to be in a place where two American families are living next to us. One is an elderly couple who are like our grandparents – wise, patient and always offering cookies! The other couple is about our parent's age with children, and they sort of fill that role as surrogate parents. It's like we have one big family in the middle of the African bush. I know of other families that are living without any sort of regular contact with Westerners, and I'm sure that's difficult. Although we have many close friends in our local community, it is impossible for them to fully relate to the world from which we came.

    Then there are days when the current state of the world can really get you down. When we do here stories from beyond Cameroon, I wish I had avoided reading the news altogether. Economic crises, global warming, plant and animal extinctions, pollution of our water and air, depletion of our natural resources, wars, rumors of wars, corruption, natural disasters causing death in unprecedented numbers and many more apocalyptic-like stories steal the headlines. It's no wonder many Christians and non-Christians alike are speaking of the end times or the end of life as we know it. Yet many continue in their greed and pursuit of money while decimating the earth despite the enormous wake-up call echoing throughout the world. The future of mankind not only relies on intelligent use of our resources, but also the decision that must be made between man and his Maker.

    Moral degradation, corporate scams, political corruption and collapse of the world economy are only a few examples of the factors causing a downward spiral that exacerbate poverty, social injustice and loss of life. It is hard to foresee a time when justice will be served and poverty ended in this life. Our only hope seems to lie in the next life, where righteousness and justice will prevail. I often find myself fighting a sense of impending doom. I yearn for another way of life that breaks the cycle of sin in which the world finds itself. A world that chooses self-interest over the good of mankind will never achieve a better world. A world that chooses self-interest over God's interest will never see a better tomorrow. We must strive to be examples to others and offer another way, the way we were intended to live. That way of life is in community, both locally and globally. In that community we are stewards of the world rather than its selfish masters.

REFLECTIONS ON SERVICE

One of the things I realized in preparing to come to Africa was that my focus always seemed to be on how I would one day serve the Lord and not on how I was serving him today. Our walk with him is a daily one and requires a God-centered focus in all we do, not just in what we are going to do. This shift in my spiritual attitude brought about a greater sense of responsibility to minister to those around me regardless of the environment in which I found myself. Until I can share the message of salvation with those in my own language, culture and country, how can I expect the Lord to entrust me with the challenge of doing the same in a world outside the one I know?

We should not expect to be given more until we have demonstrated the ability to effectively use what we have already been given. Scripturally we witness this in the parable of the servants who were each given a different amount of money by their master. Each was awarded according to how wisely, or unwisely, they invested their master's money.[5] We, too, must be productive with the gifts with which we have been blessed.

In identifying that these gifts were never truly ours to begin with, the natural result is to want to share these with those in need. Sacrifice becomes service and loss becomes gain in a world where we truly own nothing. And by "nothing", I just don't mean our material possessions; this extends to our hearts, minds and souls. These, too, belong to God, and unless we are willing to give it all back to Him, we are not truly trusting in Him. The time will come when He will ask, "Were you a wise and faithful servant, using those gifts which I have given you to glorify me, or have you been a foolish servant, holding back my blessings for selfish gain?" Which servant will you be?

Our journey to Africa has required that we give up many of those things that bind us to this world – home, career, possessions, etc. Even in doing this, we have come to realize that God wants so much more than this; He wants our all. We must be willing to give up ourselves entirely and not just our belongings. When we strip away the layers on the outside and get to the core, then we can begin to connect with our Lord in a much more intimate way. Prosperity and success can be achieved in ways completely unquantifiable in earthly currency. How can we put a value on something that has eternal worth? When we change our standard of measure, we also will find that we change our standard of living.

It seems it is all too easy to fall into a mode where I only give certain aspects of myself to God. Likewise, the same could be said for my time, energy and resources. Scripture tells us to love with all our heart, mind, body and soul.[6] That doesn't leave much to hold back. When it comes to what we commit to God, there is no line between private and personal lives, work and church lives or all the other compartmentalization that stems from a secular-driven society. I did not fully realize how corporate and consumer driven our society was until I left it behind. I felt like the chains of materialism had been broken. I also know, based on previous experiences, how quickly I can fall back into that intangible enslavement.

---

[1] Matthew 6:10
[2] Matthew 25:35-36
[3] Matthew 16:25
[4] 1 Corinthians 12:27
[5] Matthew 25:14-30
[6] Jesus replied: " 'Love the Lord your God with all your heart and with all your soul and with all your mind.' (Matthew 22:37)

CHAPTER 4

REVERSE CULTURE SHOCK AND UNDERSTANDING COMMUNITY

AUGUST 21, 2008

It's difficult to put things in perspective when your perspective changes, but there are still many experiences and encounters that serve as a reminder of the great chasm that sometimes exists between the world we live in and the world from whence we came. Some of these encounters are humorous while others are heart-wrenching. Sometimes I am filled with a sense of shame for myself and my culture. At other times I wish I could somehow incorporate certain aspects of American culture that would seemingly improve the African way of life without destroying it. I've seen how change is inevitable; the form it takes is what is of most importance.

We have witnessed how the more destructive forces of Western culture have found their way even into the most remote places in Africa. For example, let's consider the cell phone. You may be thinking there is nothing destructive about having a mobile phone, and you might even have a hard time imagining your life without one. In Cameroon, however, it has had an impact that I would consider detrimental to the health, and maybe even lives, of those who possess one. Allow me to elaborate on what I mean by this statement.

The introduction of the cell phone occurred relatively recently in Cameroon, but it's popularity has been immense in a culture where communication is of utmost importance. I am hard pressed to find many people in populated (and often unpopulated) areas without one. A decent phone can be purchased for about 30,000 cfa, or about $60 USD. The memory card is about $3 USD, and a minute of talk time is about $0.30. This may seem fairly reasonable to you considering we are in a developing country, but allow me to put this in perspective.

There are about 30 active water taps in the town we live in that are fed by the gravity water system. The <u>annual</u>

maintenance fee for the usage of these taps is around $50-$150 USD. The community taps, which have the lowest fee, typically provide for 50+ members in that community. If you do the math, that works out to less than a penny a day per person. The terrible irony is that many members of these communities will buy phones and phone credit before they will pay their "water bill". I have witnessed this first hand on numerous occasions while assisting the technicians in the collection of water fees. This is not to say similar events do not pass in the U.S. I can think of similar economic patterns in American culture. However, in America we typically don't have to decide if we will have water or a phone conversation with our best friend. We frequently have the luxury of expendable income and access to basic necessities. Such a term does not exist in an economy where there is no strong middle class and a significant percentage of the population earns less than a dollar a day.

  I see similar decisions made over other technologies that have made their way here, such as DVD's. These can be purchased at about $3 a pop even though most people don't have the equipment to play them. It would not be uncommon to hear the same person complaining their corn crop is failing because they cannot afford fertilizer for their farm at about $0.50/lb. It's not that we don't make similar decisions in the States; we have the credit machine to keep us going when we make bad investments or start living beyond our means. It's impossible to live beyond your means in Cameroon. I have often wondered what our own culture would be like if we all only lived within our means. What if we couldn't build any more of our house than we had available in cash, as is the case here? What would our family network look like if our only alternative for a loan was our extended family members? What would we invest in if there were no savings institutions, 401k plans or stock markets available to us? If the "credit crunch" continues, I won't be the only American asking these questions.

  My understanding of poverty has also been dramatically altered. There are many ways to measure poverty. We can speak in terms of absolute or relative poverty, for example. In America, we witness more relative poverty where families and individuals may not have a high household income but still have basic needs met, like running water, shelter, food, etc. Their standard of living may below the "average American". In Africa, on the other hand, we have observed more absolute poverty, where basic needs are not being met daily leading to a struggle just to survive. I have also realized other types of poverty also exist, though, and they are more prevalent in the developed world. These include moral poverty, spiritual poverty and relational poverty. Material wealth, it seems, has come at a significant cost in America. Collapse of the traditional family structure, the rise of individualism and relativism and the absence of moral absolutes are signs of these poverty classes.

I have also come to realize that measuring poverty in dollars doesn't work when trying to express living conditions. Although it may sound absolutely appalling to hear that a family lives on a few dollars a day, the power of those dollars in their financial environment is not proportional to ours. Imagine what your bills would be like if you didn't have a mortgage, built your home with your own hands, didn't own a car, television, etc., had no utility bills and met a significant portion of your food needs. This represents a large percentage of the Cameroonian population. The cost of staple foods, like fruits, vegetables, beans and rice, and many materials are also cheaper relative to what we would pay in America. In the case of home construction, for example, the majority of homes are built with mud blocks fabricated from clay excavated from a pit next to the construction site. None of this is to say that there is not significant material poverty. However, we must be cautious in how we measure poverty and how we address it. Using parameters that measure the quality of life rather than the cost of life, I believe, are more effective in demonstrating the level of poverty that exists.

Along the lines of economic disparities, the manner in which Cameroonians regard obesity is nearly the opposite of our American viewpoint. Where we stress beauty in being thin, many Cameroonians maintain an attitude of "big is beautiful". A few extra pounds are regarded as a sign of prosperity and wealth. In the U.S., we portray our financial success in our luxury vehicles or the square footage of our home, for example, while some Cameroonians choose to "wear" their wealth.

During a recent visit to the local police station for some paperwork, I was able to catch a short segment of African television. Even in a remote place like Banyo you can hook up a small satellite dish and receiver for a limited number of stations. At the time of my arrival, a Cameroonian station out of Douala was presenting this year's candidates for "Ms. Kilo". At first I thought this was an African name but quickly realized it was an abbreviation for "kilogram" as the candidates came on and proudly announced their names, where they were from and how many kilos they weighed. I don't remember seeing that on the Ms. America pageant! These women were obese and loving it. They carried themselves the same way a supermodel might because in Africa they were supermodels. I was a bit relieved to see a short segment during the show where they invited a doctor to share some of the potential consequences of obesity, such as diabetes and heart disease. I've even seen stickers here that read, "Obesity is not a sign of prosperity".

Sometimes I don't even realize how much our perspective has changed until I take a real time-out and observe what's going on around me. For example, as I'm writing this Tiffany is sifting through our rice removing any weevils and rocks as we prepare for tonight's meal. I won't even describe what the meat looks like when we go to the market. There are many other examples of how our responses to the events around us have changed, and many are much deeper than how we view our food.

Another perspective-changing moment occurred last week in our local community. During a door-to-door immunization effort as part of a government initiative in response to a recent polio case, Tiffany encountered a young boy who had a fracture in his leg that seemed quite serious and possibly infected. We learned the family had no financial means to take him to the hospital, so we decided to assist given the severity of the injury. We discovered the bone was indeed infected, and a serious condition called osteomyelitis had set in. We were informed that failure to act could result in amputation of the leg or even the boy's death. Surgery was the only option for addressing the infection.

This was well beyond the family's means, and you may think well beyond ours. We are fortunate to have a surgeon at our community hospital. He was not actually educated as a doctor in the traditional sense but learned surgical skills in a hands-on manner as a surgical technician at another Cameroon hospital. Other American doctors have seen his work and found his technique better than many surgeons in the U.S. - a natural so-to-speak. We decided we would take on whatever costs the surgery might incur due to the nature of the situation. We were shocked and relieved when we were given an estimate of 40,000 cfa for the operation, or about $100 USD. I was simultaneously saddened by the thought of how many other life-threatening illnesses or injuries in Cameroon that may have been alleviated by a mere $100 or less. My sadness deepened as I pondered what has gone so terribly wrong in our own health care system where many health services are outside the means of many average Americans in one of the most developed countries in the world.

In this world, we are kings and queens. Even when we think we have lowered our standard of living to what would be considered the poverty level in the States, we still stand out as some of the richest members of our community. It's difficult to truly understand poverty when you cannot achieve it even if you think you've found it. Mountain water piped to our home, intermittent power, extra rice and beans in the cupboard, the fact we have cupboards, a gas-powered refrigerator, a 10-year old vehicle, concrete floors – these are the things that set us apart in our community. They would do the same in America, but in the complete opposite sense. Yes, America is truly a nation of kings and queens in a world where poverty rules.

AUGUST 30, 2008

I no longer see the people we have come to know this year in eastern Cameroon as refugees. They now have names and faces; we have slept in their compounds, shared their meals, shared their pain and shared their joy. We have connected in a way that can only be achieved by really spending time in a community and experiencing life as they know it. Their stories have become our stories and our lives are now intertwined. Hope has emerged out of the disease, hunger and loss that accompanied these Fulbe families when they were forced to abandon their homes and lives in the Central African Republic. Their nomadic lifestyle and abundant cattle had made them easy targets for bandits and rebels in a country plagued by political instability and lawlessness. Now they were starting over, often merging with an existing village where some family tie existed.

Since we first visited one of these villages earlier this year, the population had multiplied five times over at that location. Although everyone was arduously working to build new homes and farms to accommodate the growing population, the resources were stretched to their limit. Some individuals were left behind in the struggle to survive and care for immediate family. In one case, a seven-year old orphan had fallen through the cracks and was suffering from severe malnutrition that would likely lead to death if something wasn't done. His condition had been identified in previous visits, but it had grown progressively worse through neglect and poor diet. Lack of protein, minerals and vitamins is very common due to a diet based primarily on starches like rice and corn flour.

When the boy was brought to the bush clinic this time, his eyes were swollen shut. He was unable to speak and instead communicated only by moans and groans. His hands and feet were also swollen, and his skin was tearing as the inflated extremities expanded. A severe yeast infection had set in around his thighs and genitalia, a sign of extreme malnutrition. Another week in this condition and the boy would probably be dead. With both parents deceased and an elderly grandmother as the primary caregiver, we identified other relatives to take him to a hospital.

On our way back through the area, we stopped at the hospital to see if we had been too late. We were overwhelmed with joy to find that he was actually recovering after a blood transfusion and improved diet. While Tiffany was assessing his condition, he looked up at her and said he would like some milk in Fulfulde. We happily obliged and thanked God for bringing us to this boy when He did. It's impossible to fathom all the circumstances of our lives that had brought us to that particular place and time so that we could provide a few basic resources that would allow this boy to live.

SEPTEMBER 5, 2008

We recently celebrated my wife's birthday. No, I didn't make a cake, but I grilled chicken, and that's a lot harder here. You see you can't just run down to the local supermarket and pick out a package of thighs and legs or one of those nice rotisserie chickens. Here the process begins by trekking into the market where you get to pick out your live chicken after an exhausting negotiation. That's only the beginning. Of course they don't butcher it for you – that's your responsibility.

After escorting the chicken home and chasing it around your vehicle upon your arrival, it is then necessary to find a nice secure place to tie it where it will crow for the next several hours before you are ready to "do the deed". You know how they say something is "running around like a chicken with its head cut off"? Well, it's true. You better hold that thing down for a few minutes. After you've boiled a large pot of water and dipped the bird, then comes the plucking. The work continues with the butchering. If you want pieces that even vaguely resemble what we're familiar with, you have to be very specific about where to cut or you'll end up with randomly cut pieces and parts we wouldn't really classify as edible. This is a process we typically have the luxury of avoiding in America. I have a much greater respect for the butcher profession.

OK, so now we're ready to cook. They don't grill chicken here, so you have to have a grill welded together by a local welder in town. You can't usually buy any charcoal either, so you have to gather firewood in the bush. After spending an hour or two making good hot coals, you're finally ready to begin grilling. Now if you want Bar-B-Q sauce, which we did, you can't just run to the local supermarket either. The nearest Bar-B-Q sauce is 12 hours away in the capitol city at the upscale supermarket. Fortunately we bought some during our last trip at about $5 for a small bottle that would last one grilling session.

So no, I didn't bake a cake, but next time I will!

SEPTEMBER 22, 2008

I have to begin this entry by adding the disclaimer "kids, don't try this at home". It involves bees – African "killer bees" as they have been dubbed in the United States. However, these are purebred African bees, the real deal. As part of our transformational development activities, we've been trying to introduce the Kenyan Top Bar, or KTB, hive. Beekeeping is a very common practice in the area in which we now live, but the traditional method is both dangerous and destructive. Cone-shaped hives made out of local woven woody materials are placed high in the branches of a tree. When the time comes to harvest the honey inside, the beekeeper will climb the tree, without any additional protective equipment or smoker, and remove the hive. They then proceed to burn the hive and all its contents, including the bees who so diligently worked to produce their sweet nectar. Although they still obtain a wonderful product in the end, the bee population is reduced and much risk of bodily harm is taken in the process.

Much of my fear of raising these aggressive bees was laid to rest last week when a local Fulbe man demonstrated exactly how much you can get away with without provoking a swarm of African bees. We recently set up several KTB hives, two of which had already been colonized. It is fairly common to hear or see a swarm of bees looking for a new home, as was the case during this particular day. In an effort to capture the bees and relocate them to one of our empty hives, our friend climbed the tree with an empty sack and began brushing the bees into it with his bare hands. Unfortunately I wasn't present at the time to witness this daring feat, but I probably wouldn't have been very approving of his method if I had been. With only a couple of stings on his hand, he walked away unscathed and with a sack full of bees.

When I showed up the next day, the bag 'o bees had been slung over one of our empty KTB hives in the hope that the swarm would relocate to the empty hive below. Unfortunately this was not the case. In fact, the bag had sealed shut with half of the swarm still trapped inside, and it was likely the queen was still in there. This called for phase two of our bee relocation operation. However, the situation had become a little tenser now that the bees were aware of an intrusion. While swarming, the bees tend to be a little more docile as they form a large mass around the queen. If done carefully, the whole ball can be moved by cutting the branch and relocating it to the hive. In this case, they had been very disturbed and weren't letting their guard down so easily.

Although our brave beekeeping friend was ready to march in unprotected, we urged him to take a little more caution this time. Fortunately I had brought some special gloves, a wire mesh hood and a smoker from the States to be used in our beekeeping efforts. After dressing him and taping all the openings of his clothing, we sent our bee soldier into the front lines. Armed with nothing but a pair of scissors, he fearlessly cut open the bag seemingly unaware of the danger buzzing around him. I don't think things would have gone so smoothly if he had not been wearing the extra protective gear. I know I wasn't willing to find out even if he was.

The concept of bee farming, or apiculture, is a relatively foreign concept in the Adamawa Province. The KTB hive would promote good beekeeping practices by both protecting the bees and the beekeeper. Multiple hives could be managed in a relatively small area instead of distributing hives throughout the bush far away from the family compound where they are also in danger of other predators. I was told by one local man that there is a large bush cat in this region that will raid hives by placing its tail in the hive hole to remove the sticky treat and then proceed to eat the honey like a lollipop. As interesting as it may be to witness this kind of activity in nature, I'm not sure if I want to get between a bush cat and his honey!

SEPTEMBER 29, 2008

More Things We've Learned While Serving in Cameroon

- ➢ We've learned how to greet people in five languages.

- ➢ We've learned that there's no second chance when you accidentally plug a 110V device into a 220V socket. Unfortunately, this lesson had to be learned more than once.

- ➢ We've learned you can get fatter in Africa.

- ➢ We've learned why goats are symbols of unrighteousness in Scripture.

- ➢ We've learned children really can be quiet in church services.

- ➢ We've learned life doesn't end when you don't have access to a phone or the internet 24/7.

- ➢ We've learned absence truly does make the heart (and stomach) grow fonder…

- ➢ We've learned we have something in common with scorpions – we both love the comfort of our home.

- ➢ We've learned it's OK when someone tells you how fat you look.

- ➢ We've learned you really do get malaria when you don't take your prophylactic.

- ➢ We've learned bungee cords don't have anything on a Cameroonian rubber strap made from old tire tubes.

- ➢ We've learned people can eat the same thing for breakfast, lunch and dinner and still be happy.

- We've learned the best way to discourage Cameroonians from asking you to help them go to America is by telling them there is no corn fufu there.

- We've learned the hard way that my wife is allergic to mango skin.

- We've learned weevils add a nice little "kick" to pasta and rice.

- We've learned we will never again desire to go off-roading in the U.S.

- We've learned cockroaches are not pleasant sleeping companions, and you should not eat in your bed unless you want to share it with mice.

- We've learned peanuts are groundnuts, avocados are pears and you don't eat them, you chop them.

- We've learned it's OK to have auctions during church as long as the proceeds go to the church.

- We've learned Gasoil is not gas, and there's nothing super about Super gasoline.

- We've learned the only way to get unbiased news about America is to leave America.

- We've learned freshly dug fish ponds make great mud wrestling pits.

- We've learned the first word that Cameroonian children must be taught is *Nasara* (white man)

OCTOBER 26, 2008

It's Sunday morning here, about 6:00 a.m. We're preparing for what they call "Thanksgiving Sunday". It's kind of like a harvest celebration where everyone brings a little something from the fruits of their labor during the rainy season as we are now venturing into the dry, dusty one. It's actually one of three Thanksgiving Sundays, so there's no lack of opportunity to give. We usually don't have any of our own home-grown produce (with the exception of some okra we're growing in the backyard with our pineapple and herbs), but today I'm considering donating one of the agric chickens, as they call them, that we have been raising.

The process of giving is really quite a riot. Everyone divides up into large groups based on where they live in the community, and then they dance in to an upbeat melody of a song leader carrying their respective gift. Then the real fun begins. In a surprisingly organized fashion, each individual item is auctioned off to the congregation. The auctioneers are usually a couple of charismatic women who serve as the auctioneers followed by money collectors and gift distributors. A table is placed in front where the money is counted openly in front of the congregation and recorded in the financial log. In Cameroon, there's a higher level of "financial accountability" regarding your giving, and they make no secret of how much groups or even individuals give. I can't say I'm particularly fond of that practice as we find it a bit awkward, but it's just another one of those cultural adjustments.

DECEMBER 01, 2008

    Our first year in Africa has come to an end, and now we find ourselves in a state of transition as we spend a couple of weeks in France prior to our return to the States. It has only been one day since we left Cameroon, and already I feel as if the experience was surreal. As I sat in the train station in Paris following our arrival from Yaoundé, I felt as if the last year of our lives had been a vivid dream. I thought back to prior travels when I had visited Africa for much shorter periods of time, and I remembered how quickly my cultural mode had changed. I remembered having the same sense of incredible distance from the world I had just left behind. This time, however, it was different. This time something had changed. This time I had come back with a mission, a sense of responsibility to those we left behind and told that we would be back to continue what we had started. This time I felt incomplete.

    I thought that perhaps I was experiencing that phenomenon known as "reverse culture shock", where the encounter with our own culture after experiencing another for an extended period of time can be similar to the initial shock felt in the foreign culture. I had already gone through these episodes during my return from Africa the first time in 2001 and again in 2005. Although I was still experiencing similar "symptoms", there was another force at work that was not adequately diagnosed as reverse culture shock. It was as I had been rewired internally. I was seeing the world with new eyes. I had a fresh perspective on the world and the role I played in it. I also possessed a renewed sense of hope for the possibility of change in the world. This time I returned with a story to tell; my own story that I felt others needed to hear to know that they too had a role to play. I had witnessed a small army of families and individuals who had shared a common vision of a better world – physically, spiritually and socially – and that army was in need of recruits. Although I had only been in Cameroon, I imagined this united army working across the globe to alleviate poverty, injustice, ignorance, corruption, disease and the multitude of obstacles standing in the way of a better tomorrow. It truly is a war, and it truly is global.

The other symptoms of culture shock are present, of course. In our case, it's a little unique this time: instead of passing directly from Cameroon to our own culture, we find ourselves in a bit of an intermediary culture here in Europe. It's probably better for our cultural sanity that we didn't rush back to the States, where life moves so quickly and we would probably be overwhelmed with extreme changes in our daily living conditions. I have always appreciated the European lifestyle and now see more similarities to the life we had come to known in Africa than I would have expected. For example, it has been my experience that the French have a strong appreciation for greetings, much like our Cameroonian brothers and sisters. Their extensive use of public transport also reminds me of our many adventures in "bush" taxis, planes and trains throughout the duration of our stay in Africa. The French and Cameroonians also demonstrate a greater appreciation for the variety of things that are edible than I recall in America.

Then there are the things that are not shared between the African and Western cultures. We had always heard a similar story from expatriates about their reaction to the supermarket upon their return to their home country. The story always included a sense of awe experienced at finding everything they needed in one store and the difficulty in making a decision when confronted by an overwhelming selection of products. The choice of which brand to choose seemed to be too much.

We, too, would now have our own supermarket story. We spent the first 30 minutes just walking around looking at things in a state of amazement. I was ashamed of my instinct to buy something because it was available to me. The onslaught of new or improved technology that had developed in only a year was hard to fathom. More compact computers and cameras, blue ray technology (still don't quite fully understand that one), more sophisticated cell phones, digital price tags in the aisles for the various products and slimmer TVs and IPods were just some of these.

When it finally came time to shop, I realized I had apparently become the most indecisive person in the world. I didn't know which box of rice to buy or which chocolate candy to savor. A trip to the store that would have taken 10 minutes prior to my exposure to the African market now was taking ten times as long as I fumbled through aisle after aisle. And how about the vendor? There was no one to haggle with over the price, and I surely wasn't happy with any of those that were clearly marked on each item we added to our basket. Maybe, I thought, we could try to convince the young guy at the cash register that they were asking way too much for the meat…

I think the orderliness, cleanliness and newness of everything is what stood out the most for me as we completed our errands in town. Although I remembered my appreciation for such things, it also made me very uncomfortable. The smoothly paved roads and lack of dust caught me off guard. Something didn't seem right. And then there was the luster associated with every car and building that seemed out of place. And why was everyone dressed in such dark clothing? Where did the sun go? Why is it so darn cold?! And then I reminded myself – culture shock, my friend, culture shock. We were simultaneously experiencing climate shock after being confronted with snow.

Now the time has come to reflect upon our experience and digest the lessons learned as we prepare for the next chapter. I was recently asked if there was a particular story that captured our experience thus far in Cameroon. I think the only way to sum up our experience is to say we can't sum it up. It seems there is so much diversity in this country in the people, the customs, the language, the climate and the landscape. The same has been true of our ministry. In this past year we have stood before kings, sat with lepers and slept with refugees. We have witnessed persecution and corruption on a level we have never known, but we have also seen love, perseverance and the Gospel expressed in unfathomable ways. I have written many stories about cultural assimilation and spiritual encounters, and, as I look them over in search of a story that would capture it all, I can only say that we came to Cameroon in search of the unreached and certainly found them in places we would never have imagined.

REFLECTIONS ON COMMUNITY

When people ask me what it is I like most about Africa, I always responds by saying it's their sense of community. The African communities I have experienced remind me of the description of the early church in the book of Acts where possessions were shared, the needy were looked after and belongings were sold to provide for the greater needs of the group.[1] This is the same type of behavior I have witnessed time and time again in both our local community and in the bush, whether Christian or not.

I believe this is driven primarily out of survival, but there is something more to it than just being in a survival mode because not all Africans are just struggling to feed themselves. At the highest level of society you find what Cameroonians refer to as "the Big Man", an affluent member of the community. In America, we have "big men", too, but there are far different expectations in African society placed on these men. They are expected to provide for the needs of the family, including the extended family, where a well-to-do American would more likely use surplus income to upgrade the model of car or square footage of the home. I have witnessed the burden placed on these individuals first-hand who struggle just as much as their poorer family members as they try to help pay school fees, medical bills and more for both their immediate and extended family.

I don't think the American community is that far away from a time when our social and economic structure was much like that of Africa. Perhaps two or three generations ago we saw a breakdown of this structure with the arrival of the industrial revolution and major advances in technology. That metamorphosis has continued until today where we find a society where the individual rules supreme and dependence on one another is considered a sign of weakness and failure.

I would dare say that the church has not escaped this change. It would probably not be unfair to suggest many look to the church to see how it can help them rather than how they can help the church and what they can get out of it rather that what they can put into it. Our individual problems become such a priority that we become blind to the world's problems. I apologize for broad generalizations, but I know I would be hard pressed to find a church in America that resembles the one described in Acts. I myself stand guilty as charged of succumbing to the mold society has established over the years for both our country and our churches. We are also witnessing the invasion of the corporate structure into the church; bigger buildings, new names, relocation, cutting staff to get "leaner", catchy slogans, emphasis on numbers, big administrative fees and other corporate-like characteristics have infected the modern church.

If you look around, though, you will see people longing for community again. Many churches have formed small groups that are much more than Bible studies; they are groups formed to reestablish that sense of lost community where accountability, dependability and relationships are being restored. People are becoming involved in each other's lives on a more regular basis rather than just a couple hours on Sunday. We are yearning as a nation for a return to our lost sense of community, to a sense of connectedness. We want to be united at times other than those when a natural disaster strikes or a national catastrophe draws us together.

There are various attempts to live in community in America that I find especially intriguing. One such case is the Amish, a Christian denomination that lives in community by promoting simple living and resistance to change, especially technological advances. I had the pleasure of being raised in an area in Michigan where there was a local Amish population. I remember seeing families driving their horse and buggy down the busy highway and selling their delicious breads on the roadside. They live in a world similar to that of the pre-industrialization era at a time when those around them live in the information age. Their traditional way of life stresses strong family and community ties. Although they may accept new technologies, they do not do it at the cost of keeping pace with them. They interact with the world around them but not in such a way that it impacts their community structure. Their emphasis on humility permeates all areas of their life and is expressed in things such as their plain dress.

The Amish are an icon for community living, but they are often shunned or ridiculed for their chosen lifestyle. What do the Amish know that has been lost by the Christian community? What can we learn from their perseverance and commitment? I think one of the greatest lessons we can glean from their example is that another way exists besides the mold of progress and individualism that has taken hold of the "developed" world. They are a living example that we can live sustainably in community without life's "finer pleasures" or technological trinkets in the midst of one of the most advanced countries in the world. When the world's petroleum resources have been depleted, it is likely that the Amish way of life will remain virtually unchanged. Perhaps the greatest lesson learned from the Amish, however, is that our dependency upon God and one another is the foundation upon which we should build our lives.

Tiffany and I also had the privilege of participating in what is known as an intentional community along our journey to the mission field. Intentional community is a term that describes a broad range of projects that involve people living together under a common vision. Our experience was in a community that promoted sustainable living through organic farming, alternative energy sources, promotion of environmental, global and social justice issues and relationships. Although their motivations were not driven by their faith, we shared a common vision for a global community and a need for change in our personal daily decisions. It was an enlightening experience and offered continued hope for a better tomorrow that was happening today.

In Africa, we became members of another type of community. Our position in this community brought with it expectations and responsibilities that were at times difficult to understand and frustrating, but in time we truly began to appreciate the sense of those with more giving freely to those with less, both materially and spiritually. The common idea we inherited from our society of "you borrowed from me and now you owe me that, and perhaps even more" is not at play in the African community. The system is by no means perfect as we often witnessed laziness and complacency that resulted from a "give freely, take freely" attitude, but, in general, at least the basic needs of all the community members were being met.

To say we gained nothing from our giving would be terribly wrong. Besides gaining credibility and trust in the community, we gained something much more than that. There is a verse in the Book of Matthew where Jesus tells his disciples that whoever has left family and possessions to serve the Lord will inherit a hundred times as much.[2] I never really understood that verse fully until I actually did it. It became clear to me in our adopted African community that I had gained hundreds of new brothers, sisters, mothers and fathers who would all warmly open their homes, lives and hearts to us because they love us and we love them. In the middle of the African bush I had learned what community could really be.

REFLECTIONS ON RELATIONSHIPS

We often underestimate the value of relationships in our daily lives. We express ourselves and our faith through our interactions with each other and our God. By focusing daily on how we interact and communicate with one another, we choose to either share or deny God's grace in our lives. Our relationships give substance to a concept that in and of itself lacks meaning. It is in our actions and words that we either glorify God or fail to glorify Him. These are the building blocks of our relationships and provide us the opportunity to demonstrate intangible concepts like God's glory, grace and mercy in tangible ways. My response to the request of the homeless individual on the street, a co-worker's unethical behavior or my wife's emotional needs are all reflections of the faith that resides in me.

In a world of broken relationships, nothing could be more important that the restoration of the most valuable relationship of all – that of us and our Creator. It is a relationship of such intimacy that we cannot fully comprehend its depth. The Lord knows us better than we know ourselves, even the very number of hairs on our head are counted[3] (not something I really want to try). He knows our needs and desires, our strengths and our weaknesses. He formed us in the womb and knew the very blueprint of our being and lives before we were made.[4] There is nothing hidden from Him, yet we are still loved unconditionally as He purposes to restore His fallen creation.[5] Love is not something God does; it is what He is. What are merely qualities we can express in our character are actually attributes of God that cannot be separated from who He is, like love, truth, righteousness and holiness.

We have but one example of that unconditional love in His Son, who gave his life as a ransom for all so that all who believe would share in the inheritance of eternal life and become part of God's family. In Christ, we are linked to brothers and sisters today, yesterday and tomorrow. The definition of this heavenly family transcends blood, tribal and ethnic relations and time and space. As part of this family, we also inherit the family business of sharing the Good News with potential "clients".

There are many positions available in the business, no unemployment, the retirement plan can't be beat and the benefits are out of this world – literally.

The greatest commands Jesus taught were to love God with all our heart, mind, soul and strength and to love our neighbor, whether friend or foe. We should seek the good in those around us and fight evil with acts of love. When we seek this unconditional love in our lives and apply it to our daily words and actions, the world transformation that we seek will become a reality. The better tomorrow will have become a better today.

---

[1] All the believers were one in heart and mind. No one claimed that any of their possessions was their own, but they shared everything they had. (Acts 4:32)

[2] And everyone who has left houses or brothers and sisters or father or mother or wife or children or fields for my sake will receive a hundred times as much and will inherit eternal life. (Matthew 19:29)

[3] Matthew 10:30

[4] Psalm 139:13

[5] He made known to us the mystery of his will according to his good pleasure, which he purposed in Christ, to be put into effect when the times reach their fulfillment – to bring unity to all things in heaven and on earth under Christ.

www.ingramcontent.com/pod-product-compliance
Ingram Content Group UK Ltd.
Pitfield, Milton Keynes, MK11 3LW, UK
UKHW041011220326
11408UKWH00001B/112